KOHOUTEK
WAS A BUST

KENNETH J. SOUSA

Printed in the United States of America.

ISBN
979-8-88945-139-6 (Paperback)
979-8-88945-140-2 (eBook)
979-8-88945-141-9 (Hardback)

Brilliant Books Literary
137 Forest Park Lane Thomasville
North Carolina 27360 USA

ONE

"I don't understand what the hell you're so nervous about, Flo. You told me your husband was three thousand miles away in San Francisco working at that Sourdough Sam place. Calm down and come over here so I can help get the rest of those clothes off." The svelte, big bosomed blond slithered across the dimly lit living room and placed herself next to her dark haired lover. As he reached his arms around to unhook her bra, a faint noise outside caused a startled look on her face and a quick turn of her head towards the window.

"Carrumba, what the hell is wrong now?"

"I don't know Manny, I'm afraid he might come home early to surprise me. Besides, I told you he can be violent. One time he hit a guy with a baseball bat who was paying too much attention to me. He also worked with the FBI to break up a drug ring. Not to mention the fact that he carries a gun."

Thinking about the adrenalin rush he felt in Vietnam, Manny boldly answered. "I told you, I'm not afraid. There's a certain rush to going out with a married woman. It's the chance of being caught." With a more soothing tone, Manny massages one of Flo's breasts and says, "Doesn't that make you feel better?" Another noise outside the window startles Flo again breaking the romantic mood. Manny loses his patience again. "What the hell is wrong now?"

"I've got to call San Francisco to make sure he's there. It'll only take a minute." Then the nervousness in her voice subsides to a purr. "After the call you can have me any way you want."

Flo's promise of sexual adventure calms Manny and he relents to her request with a sly smile. "Alright Flo, if it makes you feel better, give him a call."

As the shapely blond leaves to make her call, Manny stands and wanders to the picture window. Half drawing back the heavy curtain, he peers into the New England night. Thinking it was cool for March, he doesn't flinch as he watched a pair of headlights make their way through the sparsely populated suburban neighborhood. But he does react when he recognizes the car, and the headlights turn into Flo's driveway.

"Flo, he's home!"

At that same instant a panicked Flo rushes into the living room. "They said he left San Francisco hours ago. He could be home at any minute!" Flo freaks at the headlights, Manny doesn't. As Flo runs aimlessly between the kitchen and living room clutching Manny's jacket and screaming, "What are we going to do now!" Manny forces himself to remain calm. Flo had told Manny that her husband always parks his car in the garage when he comes home. A plan began to formulate in Manny's brain. The house was a split entry with three outer doors he thought. Lenny Solens will probably come up the stairs from the garage directly into the house. If Manny waited by the back door, he could make his escape while Lenny mounted the stairs.

Grabbing his jacket from Flo, Manny stood by the door until he heard footsteps on the garage stairs then quietly opened the door and gently stepped down the porch steps then fled across the backyard. As Manny's feet crunched through the last of the spring snow, dogs began barking and his thoughts turned paranoid. What if he saw me? What if he heard me? What if Flo gave it away with her nervousness? What if he's waiting for me with his gun when I get back to my car?! With his car in sight a few blocks away Manny began to calm and thought; the thrill of seeing a married woman, the thought of being caught. Did I actually say that? I must be crazy!

*   *   *

The incident involving Manny and Flo happened in Massachusetts in early March in 1973. At approximately the same time, a man named DR. Lubos Kohoutek, pronounced Lou-Bosh Ko-hoe-tek, a Czech scientist working at the Hamburg Observatory in Germany discovered a comet streaking through space on its way towards the sun. He promptly named the comet after himself, Kohoutek.

Soon other astronomers and scientists jumped on the Kohoutek bandwagon, and the comet took on an aura of great expectation. The dean of U.S. comet watchers, Harvard astronomer, Fred Whipple, stated; "Kohoutek may well be the comet of the century."

Down through the ages comets have been viewed superstitiously and all manner of plague and disaster have been attributed to their passing. Hailey's Comet was said to have influenced the destruction of the Temple in Jerusalem in 70 A.D., the Norman invasion of Britain in 1066, and the Black Plague in the 14th century. Writings from ancient Chinese history hinted at a comet which may have been an earlier passing of Kohoutek claimed the comet brought with it political upheaval and deception in government.

Italian parapsychologist, Astroth, best known as an advisor to well known movie people and politicians explained that comets disrupt the "psycho magnetic equilibrium" of the planetary system. He further cautioned that "human beings will be drawn to commit acts of violence, not only singly but collectively."

In opposition to all the threats of death and destruction, Dr. Karl Henize, an astronaut-scientist responsible for designing one of the instruments aimed at Kohoutek on Skylab stated; "Will the comet affect earth in any way? I'd say, only so much as it affects the emotions of the people who are looking at it."

An article in the December 22nd issue of Science News stated; "A few months ago astronomers thought that Kohoutek might have become even brighter than Venus but its later development makes this unlikely. It may however become as bright as Jupiter." In reality, the comet barely became visible to the naked eye. Thus in the eyes of scientists and the world, the great Comet Kohoutek was deemed a bust.

But was it? Or was the world looking for the wrong sparks to fly? Possibly, for as Kohoutek flew closer to the earth and sun, unusual events did transpire. In October of 1973 Anwar Sadat sent troops across the Suez Canal into Israel starting a war. In November of 1973 prosecutors in the Watergate trials noticed an eighteen minute gap in tapes provided by Richard Nixon proving "political upheaval and deception in government," and leading to the resignation of the president. Also in November, Arab countries embargoed the sale of oil to the west precipitating the first world gas crisis. That action led to the great American truck blockade due to Jimmy Carters lowering of the speed limit and a limit on the amount of gas a station could put in a tank. The president of Chile was assassinated and on December 17, 1973 Palestinian terrorists slaughtered 32 people at a Rome creating the world's bloodiest skyjacking. If that wasn't enough, on February 4, 1974 the Sybionese Liberation Army kidnapped Patty Hearst and forced the state of California to distribute seventy dollars worth of food to each person in the state. Most of the Sybionese army was killed in a fiery shootout with the police.

*   *   *

In early March of 1973, when Kohoutek was first discovered, until early June of 1974, when it disappeared from view, events on earth did take an unusual and extreme course. Perhaps Astroth was correct when he spoke of a disruption of the "psycho magnetic equilibrium."

Manny Silva, being an avid news hound is acutely aware of the extreme events occurring around the world but at this particular time Kohoutek was not his main concern. It's November 4, 1973 and what Manny is concerned about is a motion picture being filmed in his own back yard.

*   *   *

"Turn to the left Manny…Now right, not too much! Okay okay, now start moving towards the ditch."

"Growl gurrrr…." growls Manny.

"You catch a glimpse of the half-eaten body. Saliva runs in your mouth as you remember the warm blood of yesterday's kill."

"Growww gurrrummmm gurrrr…"

"Down on your haunches now…okay…now, pick up the remains of a leg and savagely tear into it."

"Gurrr mmmmmum gurr munch mmmm gurrrr…."

"You got it, but a little lustier. More savagery. More beastly! That's it, tear it apart!... Now drop the bone and grab another piece. That's it, that's it.....Now bare your fangs in a growl of satisfaction."

"growl...grumph...gurrrummmmmmmuuummmmmm..."

"Cut! Wrap it up everyone. Be back here at seven in the morning. And I don't want to hear any excuses for being late." The producer director, Charles T. Short, turns back to the monster. "Listen Manny you did great. We'll see if we can find a few more shots where you can come in as the monster. But the next time try to concentrate on what I'm saying and not so much on the growls. We're not shooting sound you know, and all that noise shit can be put in later. Okay you can give the suit to Bob over there but be ready to put it on again at seven sharp in the morning." The director then yells to Bob. "Get these bloody bones in a fridge somewhere. They're starting to stink like hell and we have to get another day's shooting out of them! And tell Sylvia I want to see her about some script changes right away."

Handing Bob the costume which changes his five-foot nine inch frame into a seven foot tall Bigfoot type monster, Manny follows the path running past the barn to the farmhouse he calls home. Opening the door he exclaims a loud "carrumba!" to a small group of people seated around the kitchen. "Little Hitler really put us through the paces today. I thought we were going to have to do that scene ten times before he was satisfied!"

The three people Manny is talking to are also members of the movie cast. Will and Rachel are both leads that Manny is letting stay at his house for the filming; the other person is Miranda Walsh.

Miranda and Manny have been seeing each other romantically for a few months now. She is a budding young actress and after he got a part in the film he talked the producer into giving her a try also. Although with what they have been going through for the past three weeks she probably isn't considering it a favor, Manny believed.

Manny got involved with the film because he is a member of the Bedford Farms Players, an armature theater group. It was the Players who Charles T Short came to see when he needed extras for his first full length feature film, Sasquatch. Manny's credits were for acting as a production assistant, did a couple of shots as the monster, got beaten up as an extra in a fight scene, and let the movie company use his house for whatever purpose necessary; including some shots in the woods of his gentleman farm.

It's November 4, 1973, Manny is twenty six and free as a bird. That is considering he is separated with two children. He has not a problem in the world, except for the fact that he owns a big old house that is falling apart and has a big mortgage. He hasn't worked since the past July when he got laid off from a high paying union construction job.

He doesn't complain. In his twenty-six years he did anything he chose. He chose to go to a state college after graduating from high school with three scholarships. He flunked out after the first semester. He chose to join the army reserves after he passed his preinduction physical. His reserve unit was activated two years later and sent to Vietnam. He chose to marry his high school sweetheart. The marriage fell apart after Vietnam. He chose to join the sheet metal union for the high pay. With the money he could buy a house, fill it with kids and live the great American dream.

The great dream lasted five years. He bought new cars, television, washers, dryers, a three bedroom ranch with a carport out in the suburbs, and had two beautiful children. With all that he should have been happy forever. He wasn't. Manny and his wife, Susan, fought. Even a year of marriage counseling did no good for their marriage. Manny had worked his way out of being a sheet metal apprentice into the head of planning. He even had his own office, but something was wrong. After Vietnam every day was harder than the day before. He could hardly keep his hands from steering into a tree as he drove to work. What could he do? He did what every red blooded American would do. He bought a bigger and more expensive house. Actually it was a farm with a barn and five and a half acres. Naturally the new house did nothing but to add to Manny's problems. He had more worries, more frustrations, and more battles with Susan. Three months after they moved into the farm house, Susan and the kids moved out.

The problem with Susan leaving did not help his job any. His work went downhill. He couldn't concentrate. Finally he asked to be taken out of the office and put back in the construction field. He thought that maybe working with his hands again would solve the disillusionment in his head. It did not. He had trouble with the outside bosses who believed he didn't want to get his hands dirty. Unfortunately the construction business began to slow down and he was laid off. What could he do now?

Manny's decision was not to do anything until he knew exactly what it was he wanted to do. He got a roommate to help pay for the farm and went on unemployment. To keep himself busy he joined the Bedford Farms Players, and had affairs with a number of the Bedford Farms bored housewives. He also began to write some pretty good poetry and started on a novel. He thought, possibly writing was direction his new life would take.

Of course the film business might be of interest too. That was one of the reasons he jumped at the chance to be in the film, Sasquatch, by Charles T. Short.

"You think you had it tough today, Manny." Miranda said after Manny's complaint while walking through the kitchen door of the farmhouse. "He had us doing the hippie food gathering scene seven times. I was supposed to be picking up potatoes or chestnuts or something and my back is killing me from doing it over and over and….."

Suddenly the phone rang breaking into Miranda's complaining. "Sorry, Miranda, I have to pick this up. It might be Charles T. He probably has decided to shoot a night scene and we will all have to go out and buy flashlights for the lighting."

"Hello….. Yes, this is Manny……Oh hi Flo……

"Say that again….He'll what? Publish my book! You're kidding! I can't believe it. …there's a letter. When can you bring it over?…..Yes, I'll be home. Thanks, I can't tell you thanks enough!...Yes, yes. I'll see you soon, Bye"

"Yaaaaaahhooooooooo!!!"

"What's going on? What's all the excitement about?" All three actors sitting around the counter asked at once.

"They're going to publish my book! They're going to publish my book!"

"Who is, who is?"

"Sourdough Sam, that's who!"

"Who the hell is Sourdough Sam?"

"He's the guy that Flo's husband works for. He owns Plebiscite House Incorporated! Flo is coming over right now with a letter from the general manager. It seems she showed him some of my writing that she has been reading and he wants to publish it! I guess he's been trying to reach me all day but we've been out on the set. I hear a car coming up the driveway now. It must be Flo. Looking out the window Manny sees Flo's car. It is her. Somebody get the door while I dig out a bottle of champagne. It's time to celebrate!

As soon as Flo walked through the door Manny says. "I can't tell you how much this means to me! Where's the letter?!"

"Calm down, calm down, Manny," Flo says. "It's right here."

***

11/4/73

To Manny Silva

Assuming, which is my first error, that the great Comet that will be here in November does not act as the first of the cataclysms- I think you have time to finish your work. When you are ready, I will publish.

As a Pisces you will probably pigeonhole this as brashness- but as a Sagittarius with a Cancer rising & moon with Jupiter in Sagittarius, I don't feel required to present further credentials then my word.

I will expect a synopsis soon, since I have no intention of waiting six months for your conclusion. It will please me to hear first before the others. You have knack that Frank Herbert does except you're trying to bring the story back home where it belongs. Only you'll know as the artist whether you'll follow up on this project; since Pisces is a weak on discipline I'm doing the most I can- sight unseen.

Criticism: Pisceans have a tendency to get caught up in the detail of their work- don't allow wordiness to hinder the flow of your communication. Like my other Pisces men you probably attach an approaching of omniscience to your work & a self-centered view of its importance. Be careful- several of us who shot out their arrows without having targets have tried the god trip & man's not ready yet. Maybe you can help him along, but you'll have to remain humble.

I've attempted to contact you personally but so far Flo & I haven't made it- if I leave without this contact it makes no difference- If you want to make contact we will. I'm in San Francisco living on a magic rock which will never sink into the sea- on my desk is a sign SUPERMAN-.

I'm learning to love all men as brothers & sisters & I'm better at it than most because I practice as well as preach. There-s room for you in my world if there-s room for the rest of us in yours. When you're ready to come to San Francisco to finish your work you have a place to stay for as long as it takes.

See you soon.

Mury

P.S. Only read some of your poems- save it for midnight communications. For now- You know your major work.

***

"The letter sounds great Flo. Thanks for all you have done.

"Are you really thinking about going through with this, Manny?"

"Of course I am. This Mury guy is going to get my book published and support me also. Why wouldn't I take advantage of it?"

"There are a few other little details you have to know about."

"Alright then Flo, give me the details."

"First off Manny, is the fact that Mury is a homosexual."

"That's no big deal, I know plenty of homosexuals. There are some great ones right in the Bedford Farms Players."

"Well the thing is. He feels you might be one too. He said he sees it in your writing. He will probably hit on you if you go out to San Francisco."

"I don't think that will be a big deal, Flo. You and I both know I love women. I'll just explain that to him. I can handle it."

"There's one more thing, Manny. He expects you to drive a rental truck from here to San Francisco with parts for the breadmaking kits. If you decide to go, you're supposed to call my husband, Lenny to set up the arrangements."

"Yaaaaaahhooo....I'm going to San Francisco!"

TWO

The buzz of his old alarm clock woke Manny at six o'clock on the day of his departure for San Francisco. Six o'clock already, Manny thought. Lenny's going to pick me up at seven thirty. That was one of the arrangements he had made with Lenny Solens a week ago. Good thing I'm all packed. I just have to shave and shower and eat my *last* breakfast at home. Huh, I sound like a condemned man. Probably didn't have to be up till six thirty or seven, but I'm moving now so I might as well keep going.

As Manny shaved and trimmed his moustache he thought of the affair he had with the wife of the man who would soon pick him up. Flo said she liked Manny better with a moustache than without. He felt it had been a wonderful affair, even if it had taken him three months to get her in bed. It had been worth it. Besides the fact that she was helping him get his book published. Half the guys in Bedford Farms would have given an arm to sleep with her. I just hope the arrangements I have made with her husband gets me to San Francisco in one piece, he thought.

It had been a week since he had talked to Lenny Solens about the plan for him to drive to San Francisco. Manny had thought he would be flown out west, but Lenny had said Mury wanted him to drive to San Francisco in a rental truck carrying breadmaking parts from Sourdough Sam's East coast factory. It had turned out that the West coast factory had run out parts to complete its breadmaking kits for Christmas orders. One of the reasons Manny had to get up early was so he and Lenny could go the truck rental company to pick up the twenty-four foot truck Manny was going to drive to San Francisco.

When he finished shaving, Manny jumped in the shower and as he lathered up he thought about Flo's husband Lenny. I wonder if he has any inkling about us. Naaah, of all the affairs I've had in the past year or so, that one was the most secretive. Too bad it had to end; it must be about three months now. Good thing it ended with us as friends. Otherwise, I wouldn't be getting published.

Manny toweled off and got dressed. Then he went back in the kitchen to fix a pot of coffee just as his sleepy-eyed roommate, Fred, came down the stairs to the kitchen.

"Hey Manny, are you ready for that long ride out west?"

"I guess Fred. I have a lot of mixed feelings about it. I told you about this guy Mury and that he thinks I'm gay. I don't know exactly how I'll handle that if he confronts me."

"You'll work it out I'm sure. By the way, when is Lenny supposed to pick you up?"

"He should be here in about forty-five minutes. I've got plenty of time to have a bite and get my contact lenses in before he gets here."

"I forgot about your lenses, are you worried about 'em on that three thousand mile trip. I would be."

"I don't think it'll be a problem. After all, I got through a year of Vietnam with them. I should be able to get through five or six days."

As he fixed beacon and eggs, Fred asked Manny if he heard about the new Arab Israeli war, Yon Kippur. "Yah, it seems Anwar Sadat's troops crossed the Suez Canal and are really giving it to the Israelis."

"I haven't heard about it yet. I guess the preparations for this trip has been keeping me pretty busy. By the way, do you really mind staying here by yourself while I'm gone?"

"No, I'll enjoy the peace and quiet without all those crazy players running around. Not to mention all the wild women."

"Sorry about that Fred, I got to have some fun in his life."

"I know. I'm only kidding. I'll miss those great after rehearsal parties you threw. At any rate what I was getting at is that war in the Mideast is already driving up gas prices. I hope you don't have any trouble getting across the country."

"Nah, Lenny Solens seems like a pretty smart guy. I'm sure he'll have it all figured out. Besides, when I sell this book I'll make enough money to pay off this house and give it to Susan, if she'll take it. Last night when I said goodbye to her and the kids she didn't show much interest in it."

Honking coming from the driveway drew Manny's attention from Fred. Manny went to the door and saw an early Lenny Solens waiting in his car. Quickly cramming in his breakfast, Manny said his last goodbye's to Fred, threw on his jacket, grabbed his suitcase and rushed out the door to meet with Lenny Solens.

Manny thought Lenny Solens to be about six feet tall. He looked in good shape and had sandy colored hair. He always seemed nervous and had quick smile of a salesman and quick answers to go along with it. Manny always felt he had to act cool around Lenny in contrast to Lenny's edginess.

As he opened the passenger door Manny got a cheerful greeting from Lenny, "Good morning Manny, how are you doing on this fine fall day?"

"I'm hanging in there, and anxious to get going on this adventure to San Francisco. How are you doing?"

"I'm doing well and Flo sends you her best. I saw how good you two were in that play 'Snow Angle'. Flo did a great job of playing a prostitute and you were great as her John. You two seemed perfect for the part."

Manny wondered if Lenny was talking about more than the two character play that he and Flo stared in.

"But enough about that silly Players group, Lenny said. You're about to go out in the real world. Speaking about real, I'm real hungry. Let's say we head down to Skips restaurant and I'll buy you breakfast?"

"Thanks Lenny, but I just had breakfast."

"Aw, come on, Skips has a great breakfast and we have plenty of time to get to Boxford. What do you say? Remember, I'm paying, or I should say, Sourdough Sam is."

Manny thought about it and the fact that he was leaving on this trip with exactly ten cents of his own money in his pocket. "Well I guess if you're hungry Lenny, I could stuff a little more in my stomach. Thanks."

Lenny and Manny drove to Skips a restaurant and lounge next to the highway that would take them to Boxford. Manny had been there too many times after rehearsals. As Lenny ordered a big breakfast for himself and a coffee and a Danish pastry for Manny. Manny tried to make small talk with the husband of his ex-lover. "I've never been in this place in the daylight before, Lenny. Usually we're here after rehearsals and they are just rolling out the vacuum cleaners by the time we're ready to leave. I've never eaten here before."

"I stop here about every day on my way to Sourdough Sam's East. I like to start my day with a good breakfast, especially with a credit card that the boss pays for. How's your Danish?"

"It's great, so is the coffee. Thanks again."

Flo told me about your writing a while back but I didn't think much of it at the time. She says you're pretty good. Mury thinks so too. Has Flo told you about him being gay?"

Yes, Manny answered in the affirmative but quickly thought, so much for small talk.

"He suspects you are too. I'm sure Flo must have told you that. But we know you're not gay, right?"

Manny couldn't help but think Lenny was talking about Flo and himself and quickly tried to change the subject again. "So, what else can you tell me about Mr. Mury W. Nestor?"

"He's got this crazy thing about the company being a family, and this idea about him as sheriff and everyone in the family has to carry a badge. See here's mine; Lenny opened his wallet to give Manny a quick glimpse of a badge. He's also deeply into astrology. Flo says you two should get along well in that department. He even had to send back to California the last time he was out here to get some special predictions from an astrology pamphlet called the 'House of Usher'. Can you believe it? Mury is all right though. He was a captain in the army and he has a degree in political science. You almost finished your coffee?

""Ya. Thanks again."

"Let's go. We got to be at the rental place by nine."

*   *   *

As Manny sat next to Lenny on their way to pick up the rental truck, Manny thought to himself. This Mury character sounds like me in a lot of ways except for the homosexual thing. What am I going to do about that anyway? I'll worry about that when the time comes. We're almost at the truck rental place now. I wonder what this truck will be like. Hope it isn't too big, and I hope I don't have to back it up often. There's the place now.

Lenny pulled he car into where Manny had seen the truck rental sign. "Manny, why don't you go over and check the truck out while I get the papers filled out. Can I have your license? I'm having the truck written up in your name. Come in when you're done and you can sign the papers."

Manny answered Lenny in the affirmative and walked over to the truck Lenny had pointed out. He thought to himself, not a bad looking truck. Glad it's a box type and not a tractor trailer rig. Still, the thing must is pretty big. Tires look alright. I hope the oil is up. The engine looks good for all I know about engines. Let me climb up inside and see how it feels. Wow, only sixteen thousand miles on the speedometer, must be almost new. Uh oh, no radio. Well, I've got plenty to think about. Five gears, glad they're marked on the shift lever. Glove compartment, log, seats wide enough to sleep on, and I'll probably do a lot of sleeping in here. Here comes Lenny. They must be ready for me to sign.

"How's she look, Manny?"

"Fine, I don't think I'll have any trouble. I told you, I drove trucks a little in Vietnam."

"That's good. Mr. Thompson here has the papers ready for you to sign."

"Just put your John H. right here son, and here's your license back. Now if you have any problems, there is a toll free number to call and here is a list of garages that we are affiliated with. The log book is in the glove compartment. That must always stay with the truck. You've got a full tank of gas so you can be on your way. Any questions?"

"Do you have any maps I can have?"

"Sure, here's one, but it's pretty easy to get out to San Francisco. Just take the Mass. Pike which is Rt. ninety, right to Rt. eighty. That will take you straight out to San Francisco. You shouldn't have any problems unless there's snow I the Sierra Mountains. In that case you'll have to get chains. Sorry, we don't provide them. You'll be able to find out from the truckers along the way whether the road is passable or not…That's about all I can tell you except good luck."

"Thanks, I'll probably need it. Oh, what about turning in the truck."

"In the pamphlet I gave you there is a list of places that handles out trucks. When you get to San Francisco just lookup the closest one and bring it over."

"Sounds okay, thanks a lot, and goodbye now."

"You all set to go Lenny?"

"Yes, why don't you follow me. Sourdough Sam's set up in a State Hospital only a couple of miles from here."

"Okay. See you there."

*   *   *

Truck handles pretty well, Manny thought to himself. I've almost caught up to Lenny. He's turning left. Got to down shift. Got it. that wasn't too bad. There's the hospital. It looks like all state institutions. Old brick buildings with tree shaded lawns, and a couple of inmates walking around. Usually there is one with a limp or a big head. Or sometimes they are waving crazily at everyone going by. Why is it so hard to look at them? Lenny said some of them are working for Sourdough Sam. They couldn't be too bad off.

Lenny has stopped. Better find a place to park.

Lenny walked over to Manny. "Manny, back the truck in over on the other side of the building. That's where we will be loading on the breadmaking parts."

"Ok."

Back it in! He's got be kidding! Where the hell is reverse in this thing? The lever shows over and down . . . . That's it . . . . . grrrrrrr. Try it again . . . . . . It's moving!

Now back down this driveway. That must be the loading bock. How the hell am I supposed to get this truck between those two walls?! Well, I'm supposed to be a truck driver. So it's time I started learning

That's it, back slowly . . . a little more . . . . scrraappee. Dam! Forward now back again . . . . that's it . . . . that's it . . . . made it! Whew. Got to hurry inside, Lenny probably thinks I'm lost. Most likely he is in a bit hurry. Lenny always seems so nervous when I'm with him. Wonder why that is?

Now how do I get in this place? I think I saw Lenny go around here. This door seems to lead down to the basement. That's where he said they put the kits together.

"Excuse me Mam. Could you tell me where I could find Lenny Solens?"

"No, but do you know where I could find a boy fren? I would like a boy fren. Will you be my boy fren? I need a boy fren! I want a boy fren!!!"

"Doris, Doris. Calm down. You'll get a boy friend as soon as you finish your work. Now why don't you go over and help David pack some boxes. That's a good girl . . . . . She'll be alright. She gets upset when there is a new face around here. You must be Manny. I'm Dick. I coordinate this operation."

"How do you do. Have you seen Lenny Solens around?"

"Yes, he's on the phone right now but he should be finished in a few minutes. Can I get you a cup of coffee?"

"Ya, that would be great. Regular's fine."

"Eeeeeeee! Eeeeeeee!! I told you I didn't want to do that anymore. I won't do it!!! Eeeeeeeeee!!!!"

Those must be attendants rushing to grab her. Not a bad looking chic. Wonder what she's doing here? Here comes Lenny. Good. Maybe I can get out of here now; this place gives me the creeps.

"Follow me Manny. We're going to have some real sourdough bread with our coffee. After that I'll show you around the place. Step right into our office here, actually it's a storage room, but it gets us away from the group. Dick's wife baked the bread. You'll like it. Have you ever had sourdough bread?"

"No."

"I guess you haven't been out to the west coast then. Out there they have it all over the place. They even sell it in the airline terminals so you can take it home with you when you leave. That's why this whole breadmaking kit thing is such a fantastic idea. People can make sourdough bread right in their own homes. You know, like wine making kits and all those things. Do you want another piece of bread Manny?"

"No thinks, I'm full."

Yuck, Manny thought. This stuff tastes awful. I hope its Dick's wife's cooking that makes it so bad. I have a feeling I'm going to eat a lot of this bread where I'm going.

"Well Manny. Ready for a tour of our little establishment?"

"Sure."

"Why don't we start over here, where Dick is supervising the packing of the kits. You see Manny because of a lack of supplies we are force to slow down for a while and all the kits aren't ready for you yet. We're working on it though so it won't be too much longer before we have you on your way. Now, right out here is our main assembly area. This is where the kits themselves are put together. As you can see, this little space over here with the desks and telephones is where we conduct the business. This is Mary White, she handles the phone for us."

"How do you do?"

"Hello."

Lenny interrupted, "Lets head back up through the assembly area, by packing and out to shipping. By the way, Manny. All twenty people working here aren't only working on our kits. They are assembling for other companies too. This is Ralf over here. He packs the finished kits in boxes of ten and prepares them for shipment to wherever the order form says. . . . . . Through this doorway the cartons are filed up so they can be easily pushed up those metal rollers and out onto the dock. You can see your truck through the window. Now down through here is what we call the catacombs, which is what is so great about this building. There is space for the storage of thousands of kits . . . . . . Yes, and this is where we store the starter. One little packet of starter can last the bread maker a whole lifetime."

"Starter?"

"Yes, let me explain. You see in the old pioneering days out west, there was a need to find some way of leavening rolls or bread when the miners or sourdoughs, as they came to be called, did their cooking. What happened was that they developed a yeast mixture to leaven with, but they couldn't come up with this yeast very easily. Especially when they were hundreds of thousands of miles from civilization. So what they would do every time they baked was to take out a cup of the dough they were making and save it for the next time they cooked. Naturally from carrying the dough around with them they got their nickname."

"So what has that to do with breadmaking kits?" Manny asked.

"This guy, Sam Mackey, Sourdough Sam, used to live up in Alaska where he got hold of some starter or sponge as it's called. As a matter of fact. The starter he began with was already seventy-five years old. He then brought the starter down to California and turned the doughy sponge into a package of dry yeast which only needs water added to become the sponge. He then started a small mail order business where he would mail out these packets of starter through magazine ads. Fortunately he ran into

Mury Nestor a few years ago and they came up with the idea for a whole kit which includes a pan for baking, a recipe book and a crock to keep your sponge in so it can be used over and over."

"Why are you in such a big hurry to get these things out to San Francisco?"

"Because, I signed this big account in Chicago for one hundred thousand kits and they have to be delivered in time for the Christmas rush. We have all the supplies we need to make our share of kits here on the east coast, but they are low on kits and supplies out in the San Francisco factory. You'll be carrying out whatever kits we have made up, plus pans you will pick up at Speningers and cheese crocks for storing the sponge which you will pick up in Illinois. We were going to have this one-legged man drive the truck but we got worried he wouldn't be able to handle it."

"I get it."

"It's almost lunch time. Why don't I finish up a few things I have to do and we'll grab a bite to eat somewhere. In the mean time, feel tree to look around. After all, you're one of the family now."

"Thanks, I'll do that. But first can you tell me where the bathroom is?"

"Sure, I'll show you. Out this way are the rest rooms. This one is for the patients and this one for us. You'll find the key hidden under this ledge over here. See? Don't forget to put it back when you're done."

"Thanks."

This bathroom looks new. They must have put them here when the basement was beginning to be used as a factor. I wonder if these people get paid for this work. Don't forget to put the key under the ledge.

It's spooky down in these catacombs. This building must be old. It has field stone walls and is musty smelling and dark. I'd hate to run into one of the patients down here. I hear screams. Must be the assembly area up ahead. Probably up this ramp.

"Look out!" Someone yelled.

Whew. Almost got hit by a load of sourdough breadmaking kits. Can't let that happen, got to stay healthy a little longer. Have to walk by those people putting kits together. I'll keep looking forward.

"Hello derrr honey."

"Would you like some candy? Have some candy."

"No thanks, bye."

Got to find a safe spot till Lenny gets back with lunch.

*   *   *

"You're right about that lunch place Lenny; they make a great steak sandwich. But the next time the drinks are on me. Unfortunately, I only have a little change in my pocket right now."

"Don't worry about it, Manny. Remember you're one of the family now. Besides, I put it on the company credit card. I'll go and check with Dick to see how the packing is coming and get right back to you. I have to give you some money and final instructions on the pickup in Illinois. Make yourself at home."

Make myself at home! Is he kidding? When am I going to get the hell out of this place!

I see Lenny coming back already.

"Listen Manny, it's going to be a little while longer so why don't we get some of the paper work out of the way."

"That's fine with me."

"The way I've got it figured, two hundred and fifty dollars should get you across the country."

"That doesn't sound like very much." Answered Manny.

"Sure it is. According to the man at the rental place, the truck should get at least ten miles per gallon. You have to go three thousand miles with a truck that has a fifty-gallon tank. Now at forty cents a gallon, it should cost about one hundred and twenty dollars for gas. Plus the fact that there is a full tank now. The tolls should only cost thirty to forty dollars more, so you have almost seventy dollars to spare. You can use that for food or whatever emergency might come along. Of course you understand that you will have to provide for your own motels."

"I'm planning to sleep in the truck, or in cheap motels."

"Well, that's up to you. At any rate, two hundred and fifty dollars will be plenty of money. Here's the money and just sign this receipt and we'll be square."

"What about the business in Illinois?"

"You won't have any problems. They are expecting you. I'll give you their address and phone number. All you'll have to do is show up there

Monday morning and be loaded up. I'm also giving you Sourdough Sam's address and number in San Francisco. So once you get past Illinois and you have any questions you are to call Mury. Any questions?"

"Go to Illinois, pick up the cheese crocks, and drive on to San Francisco. That sounds simple enough. One thing though. How do I find Eastern Stoneware?"

"I'll circle Monmouth on your map. There. See it isn't too far out of Chicago. When you get to Monmouth ask directions. It's the only company in the county making real stoneware and the whole town is built around the factory. Anyone will be able to tell you where it is. Any other questions?"

"None that I can think of."

"Oh yes, one more thing. When you get Eastern Stoneware see Mr. Mel Viceman and have him call me. There is a small financial problem we have to talk about."

"Sure."

"With that out of the way, all we have to do is finish packing the boxes and get you loaded up so we can get to Speningers. Maybe you can help us pack some boxes, and get out of here all the faster. Why don't you start on that pile of kits and I'll start on this one. I think the best way is to stack up ten, jam them in, and staple the box . . . . . . "

"Manny."

"Ya, Lenny?"

"Could you come over and help us set up the rolling amp. We're about to start loading the truck. On second thought. Why don't you go out and open the back of the truck and pull out the loading ramp. Dick, why don't you grab the other end . . . . "

Getting dark already. Am I getting out of here today, Manny thought. Back's open, ramps down, here comes the first box. Shummm. Sounds like roller skates on the cement sidewalk. That's one. Shuuuummm . . . two . . . . .shuuummm . . . . shuuummm. . . . .

"That's a hundred and eleven Lenny. Shall I close it up?"

"No Manny, we have a number of unmade cardboard boxed that have to go on. Here we'll slide them up the rollers to you. . . .shuummm . . . . .shuummm . . . . Just thirty cartons of small backing boxes and ten boxes of labels and we'll be off to Speningers."

THREE

Lenny jumped into his car and took off. Manny had no intention of falling behind this time and rushed to the truck cab and took off after Lenny's tail lights. Lenny had told Manny it was only a few miles to Speningers. Manny hoped they weren't closed. It was dusk already and the traffic was building. Lenny also said he had worked for Speningers before. He had designed the lettering on the enamel pans Manny would be driving to California. He said that's how he got involved with the Sourdough organization and Manny realized he should have asked him why he had left Speningers.

Manny prayed that the Speningers outfit was run better than the group at the State Hospital. The falling night already began telling him that this might not be the day he would be going to San Francisco.

Suddenly Lenny made a quick right hand turn into the parking lot of a Chinese restaurant and hurled his nervous self out of his car door. Manny had just parked next to him and rolled down his window to find out what was going on.

"I hope you like Chinese food. I forgot to tell you that I got a call from Fritz at Speningers. All the pans weren't ready yet. And don't worry about the prices in this place, it's on Sourdough Sam."

As they walked through the door of the restaurant, Lenny smiled over the delicious aroma wafting from the kitchen. Manny didn't. As the slid into a booth, he finally gave up the ghost of going anywhere but home that night. He wasn't happy but as usual he played cool to Lenny's anxiety. "I love Chinese," which he didn't. This was a great idea." Which he didn't believe it really was. Over a shared Pu Pu Platter Lenny explained some of the intricacies of working with the pan making company. He seemed extremely proud of what he had pulled over on Speningers.

"You see Manny; technically we should never have been able to get the credit from Speningers. We already owe them a lot of money for some of the pans they made for H&P, you know for that big account I sold out in Chicago. I had Maury send Speningers a telegram telling them we were good for the money and they had to believe it because we already owe them money and they know we have to have the pans to fill the order for H&P. Right now we're in a good middle position. It's a win win for me and Sourdough Sam's."

The Pu Pu soon disappeared from the platter and Lenny paid the check. "Let's get moving, Manny. They're probably waiting for us over at Speningers. Come on, I'll introduce you to Fritz, my old boss."

Manny didn't think the deal sounded kosher, and it sounded like Lenny was trying to put something over on his old boss. Possibly they hadn't split on good terms, but Manny figured he didn't really understand much about business. What he did know was that he wouldn't want to be on the bad side of Lenny. If he wasn't already.

In minutes they had driven to Speningers. Manny backed the truck up to the dock then met Lenny at the door where he was standing next to a short bald man with a moustache. Lenny made the introductions. "Fritz I want you to meet Manny Silva. He's driving the pans out to California for us."

Fritz had a friendly smile and Manny detected a slight German accent as they shook hands and exchanged pleasantries. When the formalities were finished, Fritz suggested to Manny that he take a look around the factory while he and Lenny go into the office to finish up some paperwork. "The paperwork won't take long Manny, but unfortunately all the pans aren't done and you'll have to wait a while wile we finish the job. So after you take a look around find a comfortable place to sit and rest while the men finish up the job."

Resigned to heading home to Bedford Farms for the night, Manny took a quick walk around the hot factory and watched the men work. They were busy painting enamel on pans, stenciling them and running them through a blazing furnace. They were then left to cool and finally piled on pallets. Soon another man would strap down the piles for a guy on a forklift who would pick up the pallets and carry them out to the loading dock and line them up behind Manny's truck. After watching for a while

Manny looked for a fairly cool place to rest and waited for Lenny to come out of the office and tell him the paperwork was finished. He found some empty pallets in a corner away from the blast furnace and sat. After an hour in more heat Manny began to nod off just when a loud beep from the forklift and a man shouted to get the hell off the pallets he needed them.

Just then Lenny and Fritz emerged from the office and headed his way. Before he even reached him Lenny shouted, "Sorry Manny there's more pallets to come, but they should be finished pretty soon. Sorry I can't wait with you but Flo's waiting for me at home. You have a great trip to San Francisco and give Maury a hug for me when you get there. He probably expects it. And don't forget, when you get past Illinois, you belong to him. I'll give my love to

Flo for you. See you soon. I'll be out there shortly. Bye now." Lenny turned and headed for the door before Manny could say goodbye. Manny waited another hour for the rest of the pans to be loaded on the rental truck and then headed back to Bedford Farms with the idea that he would get an early start in the morning. As he drove up the highway a disappointed Manny Silva searched the starlit sky looking for the great Comet Kohoutek that scientists were saying would be the brightest comet ever, but didn't see a thing. He thought to himself that maybe Kohoutek would not really be a big deal. Just like his first day on his journey to San Francisco.

FOUR

Manny was up early the next day. He felt the day before was wasted loading up for his trip to San Francisco. He was on the road just before daybreak and made his first gas stop somewhere in upper state New York. He figured the numbers and quickly realized he wasn't getting the gas mileage Lenny had promised. Instead of ten miles per gallon he was only getting five. It wasn't a good omen that the second day wasn't working out much better that the first, the loading day. He didn't waste any time finding a pay phone and calling Lenny. Collect.

Lenny picked up the phone himself at Sourdough East.

"Hello Lenny, it's me Manny."

Lenny didn't sound surprised to hear Manny's voice and he didn't sound to enthusiastic either. "Hi Manny, I didn't expect to hear from you so soon. What's up?"

"To begin with you can send me some more money." The sarcasm and annoyance in Manny's voice was lost to Lenny as a ten wheel truck barreled past the phone booth.

Lenny professed a fake surprise that Manny picked up on immediately. He was running out of patience with the game he now felt Lenny was running on him. Not hiding his anger, Manny demanded a quick solution to his problem. No answer came from the other side of the conversation for what seemed like an hour to Manny. Finally the line came alive.

"Sorry, Manny I haven't any answers for you right now. Why don't you call me when you get to Illinois. By then I'll have figured something out. Does that sound okay?"

"Doesn't look like I have much choice. I'll call you from Illinois."

"Oh and Manny, don't forget what I said about only speaking to Mr. Viceman."

Manny answered in the affirmative and hung up the phone without a goodbye.

Manny drove on until dark when his contact lenses told him he had better pull over to give his eyes some rest. Not further ahead he saw a truck stop sign and pulled in. He parked in a row of trailers and heard the growling of his stomach. He hated to spend the money but he went into the dinner for a hamburger. Then he went back to the yellow rental, took out his lenses and tried to sleep on a seat not wide enough to stretch out and froze through a cold November night.

The next morning a frozen Manny woke to sounds of ten wheel rigs pulling out of the truck stop, started the rental's engine and joined the procession. He drove all that day, switching his legs every one hundred miles to rest a foot from the pedals. By nightfall he had reached the outskirts of Monmouth, Illinois. Exhausted, he decided to stop at a cheap motel and grab a decent night's sleep and a refreshing shower. His appointment at the cheese crock company could wait until morning.

However, Sunday night sleep at the motel didn't go any better for Manny than his night along the highway. There was a constant hum in his head that made him feel as if he were still driving. To make matters worse, the motel was busted in a gambling raid. All night long there were sounds of wheels screeching, sirens wailing, and shots pow powing, as police surrounded the motel.

The next morning a bleary-eyed Manny arrived at the office of Eastern Stoneware. Lenny had mentioned that it was one of the largest manufacturers of stoneware in the country, so Manny tried to look business like as he approached the pretty secretary seated behind a mahogany desk.

"Hi. My name is Manny Silva. I'm here to pick up some cheese crocks for Sourdough Sam's Incorporated."

The pretty woman answered in a business-line receptionist voice. "Oh yes, Mr. Silva. We've been expecting you. Why don't you have a seat, Mr. Viceman will be with you momentarily."

Manny took a seat and wondered if the chick would use such an official voice in bed. His musings about the shapely girl were cut short by someone calling to him from an office door.

"Ah, you must be Manny Silva."

The driver tuned and saw a tall good looking man heading his way with his hand extended. Manny shook it and replied, "Yes, that's me, and you must be Mr. Viceman."

The tall man answered without a trace of a smile. "No, I'm Mr. Corner, Hank Corner. I'm handling this account for Mr. Viceman."

To Manny, Hank Corner's voice had an edge to it. An edge toward anger but he pressed on. "Do you have any idea how long it will take before I can load up and be on my way?"

Hank replied icily. "It shouldn't take long. The paperwork is already completed and all you have to do is sign it and drive the truck around to the dock and we'll load you up."

"Great, it's a long way to San Francisco. Oh, before I forget, Lenny Solens wants Mr. Viceman to call him while I'm here."

"Certainly." Mr. Corner motioned for Manny to follow him into his office where he placed the call for Mr. Viceman. Manny checked out the office while Corner and Solens talked salesman talk. Finally, Hank Corner handed the phone to Manny.

Lenny wants to talk to you. I'll be in the outer office when you're through."

Manny put the receiver to his ear. "Hello Lenny, it's Manny. Is everything alright?"

Lenny answered in a voice that sounded distant. "Don't worry, Manny, Hank Corner is going to give you one hundred dollars. According to my new calculations that should get you to California with no problem at all."

A feeling of doubt and mistrust crept into Manny's mind as he remembered that Lenny had already steered him wrong with his calculations. Of course, that could have been the fault of the rental agency. Giving Lenny the benefit of the doubt, Manny replied. "Good then, I'll get loaded up and be off as soon as possible."

"Okay. But don't forget, from now on you belong to Mury. If you have any trouble from here on in, call him."

"I can't see why I should have any more trouble." Then after a slight hesitation Manny continued. "Well, take it easy and say hello to everyone at home for me." The only answer Manny got was a click and dial tone.

Manny put down the receiver and went to the outer office. Not seeing Hank Corner, he went to the receptionist who informed him that Mr. Corner would meet him at the loading platform at the rear of the building.

Manny backed the rental down a pottery strewn driveway to the loading dock where he found Hank Corner with the money as promised. Without a word, Hank Corner turned and left leaving Manny with a couple of dock workers. Unfortunately for the dock men and Manny their forklift couldn't get the cheese crocks over the metal pans from Speningers so it was another three hours before he left. After the workers and Manny loaded one thousand boxes of cheese crocks over a huge pile of enameled metal pans, one by one.

* * *

Manny was on the road two hours before he saw the sign, ENTERING IOWA. Soon the plains of Western Illinois gave way to rolling hills. Then the rolling hills got steeper. By dusk, traffic had backed up behind the overloaded rental as it sluggishly moved up the slopes. To make matters worse, Manny ran into a construction area where the road turned from a four lane divided highway into a two lane highway separated only from oncoming traffic by orange plastic cones.

Feeling badly for the drivers backed up behind the rental with no way to pass as the truck chugged up the hills at a mere fifteen miles per hour, Manny careened down the hills as fast as the truck would go.

On one particular long hill, Manny managed to gain some distance from the pack. He raced down the hill at eighty-five miles per hour and was reaching for ninety when he heard a resounding, bang! Manny knew he had blown a tire and that at any moment the steering wheel would be wrenched form his hands. He waited, one second, two seconds, but nothing happened, not even the bump-bump-bump of a flat tire. Out of the corner of his eye he glimpsed an exit sign and swerved onto the ramp. He breathed a sigh of relief as a large, TRUCK STOP sign loomed in front of him.

At the truck stop Manny parked beside a big semi and got out to check his tires. Noticing that the inside tire on the right side was completely flat,

Manny remembered the words of the rental agent; if he had any trouble with the truck he was to call Ripper.

After placing the call and giving the dispatcher his location, he was told to sit tight until a man could be found to repair the blowout. Manny went into the truck stop diner and had just finished a hamburger when he noticed a small van with RIPPER RENTAL REPAIR stenciled on the side pulling up next to his disabled truck. Manny quickly paid the woman at the counter and headed for the repairman who was already pulling out a jack, tire iron, and new tire from the van.

"Hi, I'm the one who called you."

Without looking up from his work the man answered. "Where you heading?"

Happy for a little conversation, Manny answered quickly. "I'm going to San Francisco. There's a company out there that wants to publish a book I'm writing."

"That's great," he answered briskly, "but what are you carrying?"

Manny explained about the cheese crocks and bread pans.

The repairman replied matter of factly. "Well, if you want to make it all the way to California, you'd better shift that load. Those pans you're talking about are sitting smack over the rear axle. Every time you hit a bump or pothole the rear end is going to sit down on those rear tires giving you another flat.

Manny was both astonished and upset by the news. "It's almost twelve o'clock at night in the middle of nowhere. How the hell am I going to get that load shifted?"

Silently the repairman put his tools back into the truck. As he started the ignition and prepared to pull out, he turned and called curtly out the window. "That's your problem feller. I only fix trucks." He drove quickly away leaving the helpless Manny standing in the parking lot staring at his truck. Suddenly he remembered something Lenny Solens had said to him. If you have any trouble, call Mury. Manny thought a moment and made his decision. He would place his first call to Mr. Mury W. Nestor.

"Hello?" Manny controlled his voice to sound as cool as possible. "Could I please speak to Mury Nestor?"

"Just a minute please,"

A pleasant sounding woman's voice had answered on the other end. Manny felt glad there would be at least one woman out west. As he pondered this prospect another voice came on the line.

"Hello Manny, this is Mury Nestor. How you doing old buddy?"

Manny wondered how he and Mury could be old buddies when they hadn't even met, but he pushed this thought aside and plunged into the story of his predicament. After finishing his narrative with silence coming from the other end of the line, he finally heard the calm voice of Mury Nestor.

Maury suggested that Manny try to hire someone to help him shift the load. Manny readily agreed with this solution but explained the he was low on cash. Mury reassured him by promising to wire Manny money if he ran too low.

Manny's fears began to ease considerably and he felt much better until Maury said, "Listen old buddy, I've got some white stuff waiting for you when you get here, see you then." The line went dead before Manny could say, bye.

White stuff, Manny thought to himself. What the hell is he talking about? Unfortunately Manny didn't have any time to ponder the question, he had to hire someone to help shift the load.

As he hung up the phone, Manny wondered why he didn't tell Mury that he was in the middle of Iowa in the middle and there weren't exactly lots of people hanging around. He guessed it was too late for the question and figured he would just have to figure something out.

He had pulled into a truck stop; he thought there must be someone willing to earn some extra cash and started to walk towards the sign that said open, twenty four hours.

* * *

Two men working at the garage pumps both said no to Manny's request for help even if it paid. Even a group of young men drinking beer in the parking lot turned him down. Manny gave up trying to hire someone and resolved to do the job himself, even if it took all night. Which he figured it might if not longer.

As Manny walked back across the parking lot towards the truck, he looked around. All the bright moon and stars allowed him to see were flat miles of plowed under corn fields. He really felt as if he was in the middle of nowhere and he felt all really alone.

When he reached the rear of the rental he unlocked it and in the moonlight he could see the heavy pans were sitting right over the truck tires and there was no way he would make it to San Francisco unless he shifted the load. As he pondered the work that must be done he thought of Lenny Solens. He had planned this expedition and with all the problems he had so far, Manny began to think that maybe this problem was not a complete accident. Maybe Lenny was getting a little payback.

He had barely unloaded a dozen boxes of cheese crocks when he voice in the night, "Hey, Mister. I'll help you with those boxes. How much you payin'?" As the voice came closer Manny say that it belonged to a strapping young farm hand dressed in overalls. The boy looked about nineteen and was as big as a barn. Manny hired him on the spot at forty dollars, and the two men finished the job by four a.m.

Exhausted, but eager to get going, Manny packed the last box and was about to slam the door shut, when the farmhand casually mentioned yet another new peril.

"You do know that all trucks have to be weighed when they enter the state of Nebraska, don't you?"

"Weighed?" was Manny's puzzled response.

"Yah. There's a Weigh Station about thirty miles down the road." The hand hesitated for a moment. "If a truck's over the weight limit the driver has to pay a fine."

Manny considered the warning for a moment, but had already forgotten it by the time the two parted company, after all Lenny certainly couldn't plan that far ahead. Could he, Manny thought.

*   *   *

ALL TRUCKS MUST ENTER WEIGH STATION Manny saw the sign soon after he had noticed a sign welcoming him to Nebraska. Manny drove into the station and up on the scales the same as he had watched other trucks do. He didn't feel he would have any problem; after all,

Lenny would never intentionally overload the rental truck. That was until a loudspeaker squawked; "Would the driver of the yellow Rent-A-Truck park in the lot and come inside the station."

What the hell is the problem now, Manny thought to himself. He soon found out.

"You've got seven thousand pounds over the allotted road weight, son," said the Nebraska state patrolman. We're going to have to put you under arrest and take you to see the judge. That is unless you want to waive trial and pay the fine here."

"Pay a fine!" Manny was outraged in his innocence. "I didn't even know the truck was overloaded."

"That's not my fault," replied the trooper matter of factly. "You're the driver and you can't drive in Nebraska with an overloaded truck. So what are you going to do? Pay the fine or go see the judge."

Manny replied with pleading in his voice. "If I pay the fine am I free to go?" Straight faced, the trooper answered him. "You sure are. Just as soon as those seven thousand pounds are off the truck."

Manny pondered the choices for a moment. He could pay the fine that was no problem, as Mury could wire him the money once he got to the next big city. The real problem was where to unload seven thousand pounds of cheese crocks and bread pans. It seemed like time for another call to Mr. Mury Nestor.

*   *   *

This time Mury himself answered the phone. The harried truck driver explained this new dilemma and much to his surprise, Mury didn't sound upset or overly concerned. He merely suggested that Manny find a trucking company and hire them to take the overload out to San Francisco. He also promised to send more money to Manny in Lincoln Nebraska. Manny was relieved as the plan sounded just fine to him. He paid the fine and drove the truck out of the weigh station to a nearby truck stop where he began calling freight lines.

It took several calls but Manny finally got a positive response from Pick Freight Company. Directions were given and Manny settled down to wait for rescue.

Finally, a Pick truck pulled into the truck stop, and the driver opened the rental to begin unloading the goods. Unfortunately, once the trucker saw what cargo Manny was carrying his face turned red with anger and he refused to take the load. He exploded that Manny was carrying manufactured items, not household goods.

"It's against union policy for rented vehicles to carry manufactured items," the burly driver stated. "No union man is going to touch those crates, and if you take them you'll be lucky not to get your head busted open by some militant union guy. They think scabs are the lowest forms of life."

Manny quickly assured the driver that he had once been a union man himself and had no idea it was against the rules or he wouldn't ever have taken the load. As he was about to continue his explanation, he noticed that the green-lit sign announcing that the weigh station was OPEN had changed to CLOSED.

An idea began to take form in Manny's mind. If this station closed, so must all the others the farm boy had warned him about. All he had to do was drive to the next station and wait until the sign changed from open to closed, and then barrel on through. A sense of euphoria swept over him. He could make it after all.

Quickly he said goodbye to the Pick man and thanked him for the warning. On impulse he ran to the telephone and placed another call to Mury Nestor. "Listen, I've got it all figured out. I'm taking the load out myself. Nothing's going to stop me now. Watch out, I'm coming through!"

WEIGH STATION OPEN

Manny sat in his truck on Interstate 80 somewhere in the middle of Nebraska, waiting for the brightly lit OPEN to change to CLOSED. He had cleverly put our markers to indicate that his truck had broken down, just in case some state trooper decided to investigate. Unfortunately, his scheme backfired on him as a trooper did investigate and then insisted on taking him to the weigh station so he could call the Ripper Company for help.

Standing between two well meaning state troopers, Manny was forced to call Ripper and invent some story about smoke pouring out from under his dashboard. Elaborating a little more for the sake of reality he went on, "I just didn't think I should continue on my way without having a mechanical check-up."

Resigned to his fate, Manny passed the time waiting or the repairman by telling the troopers of his life and the good fortune that had befallen him regarding the publishing of his book. By this time the truck showed up and towed him right past those weigh scales. Manny waved a happy goodbye to his two new friends, who returned his wave and shouted, "Good luck."

By now Manny was even more determined to make it to San Francisco. At the repair garage, Manny quickly invented another story by looking under the dashboard and assuring the repairman that he had discovered some crossed wires which must have accounted for the smoke. Jumping in the truck, Manny turned on the ignition and was off.

Even the sight of another weigh station couldn't stop Manny now. He rolled straight over the scales without stopping for a breath and cruised over the state line and into Wyoming. He ducked off the Interstate only once, and then just long enough to make sure he wasn't being chased.

He was nearly to the Sierras, whistling "San Francisco Here I Come" when he was stopped for the last time. This time he was told he would have to put snow chains on his truck or he wouldn't be allowed to cross the Donner Pass. Manny said he didn't have enough money to rent the chains, but the guard was firm. Manny implored the man once more and when this failed, he floored the pedal and sped on up the mountain leaving the angry guard yelling after him, "You'll never make it."

Nothing could stop him now. He skidded the truck up the mountain and slid it down the other side. He sped towards San Francisco like a man who had a rendezvous with destiny, totally oblivious to the fact that the great Comet Kohoutek was also speeding towards its destiny.

FIVE

Following the directions Mury had given him when he stopped to call from the Bay Bridge, Manny parked the truck in front of a school on 30th Avenue. He estimated that it must be nearly midnight. It had taken Manny six days to cross the country, but he made it. He was in San Francisco and across the street was a sign, SOURDOUGH SAM'S FACTORY AND GENERAL STORE.

Mury had told him he lived in an apartment above the factory and as Manny looked up he could see a light shining through a large bay window. A head, which he assumed belonged to Mury, was framed in the light. Manny locked the rental and crossed the street towards a door which looked like an entrance to the upstairs apartment. Pausing to take a deep breath, he prepared himself for his first face to face meeting with Mr. Mury W. Nestor.

A buzz greeted his ring and the weary driver opened the door to a small hallway with stairs leading up. A strong friendly voice rolled down from the landing above.

"Hi, come on up."

Manny looked up trying to follow the sound, and had his first real look of Mury Nestor hovering on the landing above. First Manny noticed the smile, then the bottle of champagne, and finally the largeness of the man. As Manny climbed the stairs, more of Mury came into focus. He had sandy colored hair worn parted on one side. Manny thought it looked sculptured to fit his head. Below his hair was a wide forehead, broad cheeks and a strong chin. His nose was small and his eyes were piercing like his smile. Flo had been right about Mury's good looks.

As Manny reached the top landing he noticed that Mury Nestor had a husky build, broad shoulders and long arms that ended in a pair of strong hands which were in the process of pulling the cork from the champagne bottle. His back was ramrod straight and the pair of shorts he wore revealed powerful legs and thick tight flanks. Manny could see only the slightest bulge around his middle.

Ushering Manny into the living room, Mury immediately introduced him to an enormous green plant named Charlie according to Mury, which hung in the bay window. Mury then quickly disappeared into another room for champagne glasses. Cautiously Manny looked around the room trying to find an easy escape route should it become necessary. He also tried to get a feel for the man who had brought him to San Francisco.

Standing in the doorway in the center end of the rectangular living room, Manny looked to his right. In front of the bay window and directly under the hanging plant, was a well used sofa. To his immediate left was a macramé planter suspended from the high Victorian ceiling and hanging almost to the shinny hardwood floor. The planter was hung conspicuously next to a flickering gas lit fireplace. The other side of the fireplace was occupied by an enormous bookshelf made from boards and concrete blocks. One shelf was taken up by a stereo playing a Janis Joplin album which blared through two large wooden speakers. Another shelf held stacks of albums and an odd assortment of books.

At the other end of the room was a card table with an assortment of knicnacks. In front of the sofa was another hand-made piece of furniture; a chunk of triangularly shaped plywood standing on more cement blocks. A small television sat atop this makeshift, but attractively stained table, and appeared to be the only thing holding the plywood down. Across from the table was a bentwood rocker next to the door Mury had disappeared through.

He then turned back to the table and Manny's eyes caught sight of another item on the table. A clay pipe similar to one that George Washington might have smoked. As if reading his mind, Mury called from the next room.

"Why don't you fill up that pipe on the coffee table with some dirty dope? You do like to smoke marijuana, don't you?"

His voice was pleasant but also commanding and Manny wondered if Flo or Lenny told Mury he smoked pot. If either of them announced that fact, what else might they have mentioned? Like maybe the fling between he and Flo. Reaching for the pipe, Manny called back through the door, "I'd love to but where do you keep the stuff?"

The voice from the other room replied something about a wooden box over on the bookshelf. Manny found the grass easily, stuffed the pipe full, and sat waiting with uneasy anticipation.

A short while later, the two men sat in awkward silence as they passed the clay pipe between the rocker and couch. Between each pass they sipped champagne and eyed one another. As Janis Joplin ended and Pink Floyd's "Dark Side of the Moon," slid onto the turntable the silence grew heavier. The heartbeat on the album seemed to match Manny's own as the smoke began to mix with the hum in his head from the three thousand mile drive.

Finally, Mury broke the silence. "I decorated the apartment myself. I even made the macramé planter. How about some more champagne?"

In Manny's mind, Mury's tone implied that he obviously had a flair for it which reminded him of Mury's homosexuality. Not that Manny felt he had anything against homosexuals but he never seriously encountered one and he was wary of all Mury's moves. The only thing he could do was hold out his glass as another road driven hum roared through his head. Quickly he tried to clear his mind in case Mury attempted to put any moves on him.

As if reading his mind Mury asked, "Would you like to see the rest of the apartment?"

"Sure." Manny tried to make his voice sound nonchalant. As he rose and followed Mury into the next room, Pink Floyd's Dark Moon crashed into its full melody.

First, Mury led him into a room he called his "private office." It was a large square hallway furnished with desk, chair, a masculine looking dresser and five doors: one which they had just come through, one which led to a closet, one to the kitchen, one to the bathroom, and one to the bedroom. To Manny's relief, Mury chose the door to the kitchen.

The kitchen was tiny and had just enough room to hold a sink, stove and counter. One wall was filled by a large glass cabinet holding utensils, dishes, and huge ceramic bowls, the likes of which Manny had never seen. Manny also noticed a door which led out to a roof deck. Mury said he had it set up like a patio, complete with lounge chairs and a garden table.

As they re-entered the private office, Mury paused briefly as if lost in thought, before entering the bathroom. Here Mury pointed to a poster hanging over the toilet and explained that it was a representation of his Sagittarius sun with Cancer moon and rising. Reaching in front of Manny he flipped open the medicine cabinet revealing shelves overflowing with every imaginable variety of vitamins. "These keep my friend Bobby and I youthful and energetic," Mury exclaimed with a salacious grin.

"Exactly how old are you?" Manny said stalling for time. "Thirty-one but I don't feel a day over twenty five."

"Come on, you can't be." Manny was still trying to avoid a tour of the last room, the bedroom.

With a few quick steps, Mury was out of the bathroom and pushing open the door to the bedroom. Manny, trying to act cool and not show his nervousness, glanced around the room. It had the same high Victorian ceiling as the rest of the rooms, except this one was painted dark blue which contrasted nicely with the royal blue of the walls. Large un-shaded wood windows overlooked the patio Mury had mentioned in the kitchen. Then he pointed out a door on the right which he said led to a small porch and beyond that a door to Sourdough Sam's private apartment.

Attempting to keep the subject light, Manny asked, "When do you think I'll get a chance to meet him? Flo told me he's quite a character."

"I don't know. He's out of town on a big promotional campaign for the breadmaking kits. He'll probably be gone for some time."

Mury continued his tour pointing out a large black Ben Franklin stove which he said ran on gas, and waved at two more large wooden speakers. The speakers hovered over a cluttered dresser which included a strange plant that Mury described as a sensitivity plant.

"This plant's my favorite plant." As if to prove his point, Mury gently touched the delicate fronds which responded by folding in on themselves.

To Manny's chagrin, Mury finally mentioned the bed. It was covered with a beautiful quilt Mury said was made by his wonderful aunt. Abruptly, Mury ended the tour by asking Manny if he'd like some more champagne and dirty dope in the living room. Much relieved, Manny followed him out of the blue colored room and back to his seat on the couch. With the bubbly poured and smoke pouring from the clay pipe passing between the somewhat strangers, Mury announced it was time for the special "white stuff" he had promised Manny on his arrival to San Francisco. Manny, anxious to finally have the "white stuff" mystery solved, watched as Mury took a round shaving mirror, a razor blade, and a small piece of tinfoil from the bookshelf.

"Do you like cocaine?" Mury eyed him carefully.

"I've never tried it," was Manny's truthful reply.

Suddenly a large smile appeared on Mury's face and his eyes seemed to bulge in disbelief. With a tone leaving no room for disagreement he said, "You're going to love it."

Fascinated, Manny watched as Mury took some crystals from the foil and placed them on the mirror. Taking the razor he proceeded to chop the crystals into a fine powder. Next, he produced a one hundred dollar bill from his wallet and rolled it into a straw with a side comment that to use a smaller denomination just wasn't proper. Deftly, he drew out two thin lines of the cocaine. Handing both the straw and the mirror to Manny, he instructed him to sniff both of the lines into his nostrils. Following the directions Manny sniffed a line of the cocaine into each nostril.

He had barley finished the task when Mury said, "There's a little left, get it all."

Manny complied with the instruction. Far back in his nostrils he began to feel a swelling and a slight burning sensation. Something bitter tasting dripped into his throat. His stomach began to feel a little nauseous and he swallowed hard to keep from vomiting. In his mind Manny thought this was the last straw. How far was Mury going to take this seduction routine? I'm not into men. Suddenly he felt defiant. If he could cross an entire continent, through cops, through teamsters, through blizzards, I'm not going to do something I don't want to do, now. Not even to publish my book. All these facts raced through his mind, until suddenly his thoughts stopped.

All at once he relaxed and began to feel very good. The cocaine and pot buzz was blending with the hum in his head from the trip. Dark Side of the Moon had started playing again, and bells had started ringing through his body. Glancing at the clock on the bookshelf he noticed it was two a.m. He hadn't slept decently in almost a week and yet he didn't feel tired. He felt as if nothing in the world could bother him again. Suddenly, he was pulled back to earth by a questioning voice.

"Silva, that's a Portuguese name, isn't it?"

Manny nodded yes.

"Where'd you get those big blue eyes, then?"

"I'm half English, half Portuguese. I like the combination. It gives me a cool English exterior with a hot Latin interior." Manny heard the words come from his mouth and hoped Mury wouldn't take them the wrong way.

"A hot-blooded Portagee', huh? From what Flo tells me, you pretty much live up to that image back in Massachusetts. "

At the mention of home, Manny told Mury that he also had an ex-wife and two children. Then, as the coke began to take firm hold, the conversation began to quicken.

Mury told Manny his parents, a sister and married brother lived near Sacramento, and if Manny had wanted to he could have stayed with anyone of them that night instead of pushing on to San Francisco.

"I was truckin' and nothing could have stopped me from reaching Frisco tonight."

Mury informed Manny that the native San Franciscans didn't care for the nickname, Frisco.

"What about the possibility of an earthquake?" Manny imparted his fear to the other man.

Mury told him he too, had those same fears, but felt there was so much good energy pouring through the city that it was worth living there, earthquakes or not. Soon, with the cocaine racing through them, the two men began to relax with each other and the conversation about earthquakes turned into one about cataclysms.

Manny explained that he believed some form of geological event, such as an earthquake or tidal wave, might be caused by bad vibrations of the populace or possibly by the passing of a comet like Kohoutek.

Mury explained his feeling that a number of people would survive this type of holocaust, and he intended to be one of them. He explained how he felt it was his duty to shoot out as much energy in as many directions as possible in order to take as many survivors of the holocaust with him. "I've set up this Sourdough Sam organization for that very possibility. I've organized the whole system along family lines, so that when and if the cataclysms' do come, I can take the group along with me and we'll already have a means of survival. I can even use the same financial structure to re-organize the world. Sometimes when I start thinking about it, I feel that I'm already living it."

As Manny listened to the serious tone of the man's statements, it became clear to him that Mury took this business about cataclysms as seriously as he himself did.

The two had more wine, pot and cocaine while Mury explained how the Sourdough Sam organization worked. "Everyone who works for Sourdough Sam is part of a family. The company not only pays you a salary, it gives you a line of credit up to a certain limit. In some cases, it even provides an apartment and car. The whole family set-up can be used after the cataclysms.

At the mention of the words cataclysm, Manny jumped right in again explaining to Mury how he had read in an article in TIME that a group of five thousand people in Chicago were working together to learn crafts so they could survive the floods and other dangers that would inevitably follow the disaster. He told Mury that he felt that southern Illinois was the place people should go, and stated that he read that Edgar Cayce also felt southern Illinois was the best place for survivors.

Mury spoke up immediately. "I read that the Mormons plan to go to St. Louis after the cataclysms strike. St. Louis is right across the river from southern Illinois. Come to think of it, I remember reading in this book by a man named Ignatius Donnelley that at one time the world was hit by a comet in the Atlantic Ocean, and the splash of mud it threw up covered all of the eastern half of the continent, except for southern Illinois. Maybe the place is sacred?"

Manny came back just as quick. "And I read that a group of people in Chicago are building a rocket ship to escape the devastation of the cataclysms. They're building it in southern Illinois.

The two men stopped talking and stared at one another. They both realized their minds clicked tin the same direction. Mury broke the silence again. In an Irish brogue that Manny would come to recognize as a change in direction, Mury said, "Well me boy you must be famished from your trek across the country. Why don't we meander down to the deli for a snack? Manny thought a moment, in his hurry to reach his detonation he hadn't even stopped for breakfast.

Before Manny could make up his mind, Mury jumped up with the enthusiasm of Teddy Roosevelt taking San Juan Hill and exclaimed, "We're going to raid the Deli!" Manny was instructed to wait until he grabbed another bottle of Champagne and the two new friends went through a closet door which led to stairs down to the factory. Switching on lights as he went, Mury made his way through the maze of unmade Sourdough breadmaking kits in various stages and also boxes to pack them in. Mury explained the Sourdough operation as they went. When they reached the office area, it was separated from the rest of the warehouse by a high wooden counter. A long triangular name plate sat in a prominent position. It had one word on it, SUPERMAN. The only other outstanding artifacts were an old square safe and an antique rocker. The rest of the office area was filled with the necessary equipment to run an office.

Manny followed Mury through an archway and as more lights began illuminating the area. Manny then came face to face with a glass fronted refrigerator.

Mury explained that this was Sourdough Sam's General Store and Delicatessen. Imported hams, roast beef, turkey, cheeses, and a variety of prepared salads stared back at Manny. A few tables covered with checkered cloths dotted the area. The shelves in the store were filled with knickknacks, old-fashioned cookware, antiques and cheese crocks like those Manny had just carted across the country.

Running his hand over the smooth chopping block, Manny noticed a long counter to his left. Assorted teas, an antique cash register and jars of penny candy were lined up neatly along the top. Directly behind them were a coffee grinder and several canisters of coffee beans. Labels that Manny had never heard of were written on the front: Java Mocha, Columbian Dark, and Venezuelan Blend. Looking around Manny felt like a kid in a candy shop.

All at once Mury began hauling chunks of meat out of the refrigerator. Unsure of what they might be, Manny warned Mury that he didn't care for spicy or fancy foods. "A plain turkey sandwich with mustard is fine for me."

Complying with his request Mury produced a sourdough roll, slapped on some turkey and slathered on mustard and dropped it on a plate. Then he proceeded to make for himself what looked to Manny like some strange hybrid version of a hero sandwich. Mury popped both sandwiches into a microwave oven. A few minutes later the bell rang and Mury announced dinner was served.

He grabbed two kosher dills from a big pickle jar and indicated Manny should follow him back to the office. Putting the masterpieces on the counter, Mury pulled up a chair for himself and told Manny he could have Mury's own special antique rocker to sit on. Manny began to feel Mury held a reverence for anything in his apartment or the factory, almost as if the objects weren't simply furnishings, but sacred objects in a church.

After his first bite, Manny realized he was famished and he quickly wolfed down the sandwich and pickle. A belch involuntarily escaped him and after a moment's digestion he was ready to pick up another conversation. Soon Mury finished his meal and the would-be author and the "new wave" business manager were off on a discussion about the "bomb."

Mury believed the United States should flex their muscles more in dealing with other countries. "Tell the Russians and Chinese to watch their step or we'll blow the fucking bejeezez out of them." He pronounced the 'ing' sound strongly when he used the word fucking. As if to validate that he knew what he was talking about, Mury informed Manny that in addition to having been a captain in the army, after only four years, and a company commander in Korea, he also had a degree in political science from the University of Denver.

Manny barely heard him as he went off on his own tangent. "You see, I think that our generation is on the verge of revolt. It's no wonder too, when you think of how influenced we've been by living under the constant threat of total annihilation."

"Jesus H Christ, Manny, what does that mean?"

Manny's generally low nasal toned voice jumped to a high pitch with excitement. He sounded like Richard Crenner sounded when he played on the TV show, Our Miss Brooks.

"Mury, just think. Every other generation up until now only had to deal with an uncle, or maybe a brother or father, going off to war and possibly dying. Now a whole generation has grown up with the knowledge that the entire earth and them with it, could be blown to bits at any second. It's no wonder there's a philosophy of live for today and not tomorrow."

Before Mury could offer an opinion, Manny was off on another subject, the Vietnam War. Being a veteran of the war, Manny felt that his opinions were the gospel truth.

"I've been following the Vietnam situation since early 1960. It's my conclusion that due to the "big red scare" after World War II, the overwhelming feeling in the country was that Communism had to be contained. People were scared so we set up NATO in e, Europe and SEATO in Asia with war machinery that would start moving if buttons were pushed by Communist aggression. When it appeared the aggression was taking place in Vietnam, the machine went to work. The only trouble was that by the time of the Vietnam War, most people in the United States had forgotten they had set up the machinery, SEATO, and all of a sudden they were asking where the hell had this war come from. They didn't realize that there's always a Pentagon and Military Industrial Complex whether it's visible or not."

As Manny paused for a breath, Mury suddenly offered a toast. "Here's to you and your beliefs." The two men drank and Mury launched another topic, his theories on energy.

"I feel that energy shoots out in all directions." As the man spoke, Manny watched him in silent fascination.

Each time Mury mentioned energy; it seemed as if energy itself was shooting from his eyes. Manny listened as Mury used words like infusion, suffusion, input and output. From energy, Mury moved on to a more personal subject.

Apparently he was raised as an Army "Brat" and had lived in places like Germany and England. He told Manny that as a child he had been a little fat kid with glasses, just like Piggy in Lord of the Flies. Now, he kept his body in shape by playing ping pong. As the man spoke, Manny noticed his hands moved in a flowing motion. He had a sincerity and truthfulness about all he said and yet while Manny wanted to like him, he felt on the defensive when Mury began talking about himself as if he were Superman.

Manny certainly didn't feel that way about himself, and he felt he had to stay on equal footing with this fascinating new friend. Searching for some comparison to equal Mury's accomplishments, Manny said he too, had built a family back in Massachusetts. He had found a group of people who were interested in what he was doing and together they were constantly looking to the future and what it might hold. He mentioned that most of these people were women.

Mury didn't appear to have much regard for women. Manny proceeded to attempt a change in his opinion by telling of all the women he knew, their accomplishments, and how he felt that women were actually the stronger of the sexes. "They're more sensitive and seem to stand stress better. Besides, more female babies survive the trauma of birth."

Mury seemed unimpressed by this lecture on the virtues of women and countered with stories of all the wonderful men he knew. A rivalry between the two men had developed.

Mury took the difference of opinion one step further, extolling not only men, but homosexuality, "Sourdough Sam would give his life just to be able to get his little finger up the ass of my friend, Randy. Yet that fucking Randy always denies there's anything between him and me."

Here was the chance Manny had been waiting for. "Personally, I would never get involved in a homosexual affair. I believe that women present many more openings, physically as well as psychologically. Men are literally, too hard."

"Women are all ball busters," Mury countered, "They only want to emasculate men and use them for their own selfish means."

"I couldn't disagree more," Manny argued. "Women are strong and sensitive and can more readily perceive that the world needs a new order."

Breaking in, Mury stated, "Men might very well be slaves to that new order and anyway, women wouldn't have the brains to make a new world order."

The battle between male and female went on for some time and with each round; Manny felt the conversation was leading to a confrontation between him and Mury over Manny's sexual preferences. The two men sat in the dimly lit warehouse, face to face, arguing to the point where it became clear that no capitulation or resolution could be reached. Almost at the same instant, each ceased talking, both out of breath. The silence was electric until Mury broke it with a new topic.

"I have a special project coming up. I'd like you to be in on it." The tone Mury used reminded Manny of the way he had mysteriously mentioned "white stuff" over the telephone.

"What is it?" Manny was suspicious.

"I don't want to go into the details now," then with a pause, "Well; I guess it's time for bed."

Casually, Manny asked, "Where can I sleep?"

"In my bed," Mury replied with a rakish grin, "There's nowhere else."

"I'll sleep in your bed, but, all I'm going to do is sleep," Manny replied with determination in his voice.

Mury consider Manny's statement for a moment and seemed to accept it. "Of course, me boy, you've already stated that you're not interested in men."

In Silence, the two men went back upstairs, through the living room, past the private office and into the blue bedroom. Immediately Manny took out his contact lenses and stripped to his shorts and tee shirt.

Just as Manny was pulling back the sheet and preparing to jump into bed, Mury, who had been watching him from the doorway, caught Manny off guard. "Nobody sleeps in my bed with anything on, take off the rest of that shit, Silva."

Manny knew it was time for the real battle and he knew Mury was just letting himself in for a big letdown. He had pushed his way across the country by sheer force of will and sheriff or superman or whoever Mury thought he was, would not bend that will now. "Okay, if you insist but I'm still not doing anything." Manny shed his under clothes without protest and climbed into the big bed.

He tried to relax but he wasn't the least bit tired, even though he knew he should be exhausted. He wasn't feeling the dope anymore but he still had the constant hum of the road running through his head.

Manny felt Mury get in the bed beside him. The two men lay quietly for a moment and then it started. At first, it was the slightest touch as Mury moved closer and the two bodies met. Manny felt the hand, hard and cold and very masculine, trying to massage him. Pushing the hand away, Manny mumbled something about having to get some sleep.

"Okay," without complaining Mury complied with the request and rolled to the other side of the bed.

Manny closed his eyes for what seemed like five or ten minutes while he tried to control the hum in his head which made him feel as if he were still racing down the highway. Then, he felt a foot. Unable to respond or protest, Manny lay frozen in his spot. The foot began to brush up and down his leg. Finally, Manny managed to rollover presenting Mury with his back. Suddenly he felt a hand near his ass, Manny quickly turned on his back. Out of the corner of his eye he could tell Mury pretended to sleep while he slowly inched his way closer to Manny. Manny wondered what time it was but decided it didn't matter. It was apparent he wasn't going to get any sleep, but neither was Mury.

Gazing out the big window to his left, Manny watched it getting lighter outside. All at once an arm rolled over him. Pushing it off roughly he snickered, "I told you I wasn't going to do anything."

"I know, I know," Mury replied sarcastically.

For a while there seemed to be no new assaults and as Manny lay there, half asleep, his mind began to wander. Thoughts of Chicago, Iowa, Nebraska and his kids back home were silenced as one last hum rolled through his head. Slowly he began to lose consciousness.

He didn't know if he was awake or dreaming, but suddenly, Manny felt as though his limp prick was surrounded by moisture. It wasn't long before reality pulled him awake.

In the dim light he could see Mury bending over him and sucking his cock. Manny rolled to his left side trying not to let on that he was awake but Mury held on. Manny then tried to roll back on his right side, but Mury had most of his weight on Manny's lower extremities. In order to move, Manny had to pull his legs up under him. When he felt he had the leverage he needed, Manny made one quick movement using all the strength he had from years of construction work and lifted Mury off of him.

The move caught Mury by surprise, causing him to lose his balance. With arms flailing, he sailed off the bed and onto the floor.

Although the sight of the man on the floor tempered Manny's anger, he couldn't stop himself from saying, "I told you so." Then, he broke into uncontrollable laughter.

Mury muttered something about Manny meaning what he said, and to Manny's relief, he noticed that Mury was laughing too.

SIX

Manny had no idea what time it was when distant voices woke him up, but he felt as if he hadn't slept at all. Sunlight streamed through the window and he rose to see what San Francisco looked like in the daylight. Soon he realized the voices that woke him came from somewhere in the house and upon hearing the rattle of pans; he knew they came from the kitchen. Along with the voices and rattles he could make out the sound of something being beaten in a bowl. One voice he recognized was that of Mury Nestor.

That same familiar voice called out to him. "You want some coffee, Manny?"

"Yes please," Groggily Manny replied. He could hear Mury speaking to another voice, an unfamiliar one.

From the kitchen Mury's voice boomed again to Manny. "By the way, this little turd in the kitchen with me is Bobby. He's my secretary and he's making us some sourdough pancakes."

"Hi Manny," a lilting voice called out from the kitchen. It sounded like a young voice and it lilted to the bedroom again. "I hope you like pancakes?"

"Sounds great," was Manny's reply, hoping that sourdough pancakes were better than the sourdough bread he had sampled already. Manny could hear Bobby's lilting voice saying something to Mury, but the conversation became inaudible as still another roaring hum ran through Manny's head. His body still felt as if it were speeding down the highway. He decided to take a shower and wash his hair to try to slow the feeling down.

By the time Manny had finished his shower, Mury had gone down to the warehouse to supervise the unloading of the rental truck. Manny's suitcases had been sent up and after running his hand over his face Manny opened the suitcase and found his razor. After shaving, Manny changed to some clean clothes before venturing out to the kitchen to meet the owner of the strange lilting voice, Bobby.

Bobby greeted him cordially. He was very boyish looking and dressed in tight cord jeans, a tight jersey shirt. A pair of small brown boots covered his feet and matched his short brown curly hair. His face looked elfish, a trait Manny always associated with Capricorns. Mury had already explained that Bobby was gay, but had emphasized he wasn't gay in a "Nelly" way. Bobby looked effeminate to Manny, but he figured that "Nelly" and effeminate must be two different things.

As Bobby cooked, he and the newest arrival to Mury's family, talked of Sourdough Sam and Mury. "Mury is just a fantastic person," Bobby lilted to Manny as he flipped a pancake on to a waiting plate.

Trying to be friendly Manny asked Bobby how he liked working for Sourdough Sam.

"I like it," he answered after some thought and added, I worked here once before but there were a few problems. Bobby didn't explain what the problems might have been. He continued. "I'm sure everything will work out this time," he said as he placed a heaping stack of pancakes on the table. Staring at the enormous stack in front of him Manny asked, "Am I supposed to eat all of those by myself?"

"Of course not, silly," the lilting voice answered with a giggle. "Ned, the guy in charge of production and shipping is coming up for breakfast. Mury often has people who work for Sam's up for food, or smoke and drinks."

Manny wondered how many he also had up for bed and if everyone working in the place was gay. Bobby excused himself and went to call Ned to breakfast.

It seemed as if Bobby had just hung up the phone when Manny heard someone coming up the back stairs. As the door opened, Manny was greeted by a man with an open friendly looking face.

"Howdy," the greeting was warm with a hint of Texas accent, but the man seemed shy as he gave Manny a warm firm handshake. The two men sat in silence over the pancakes for a few moments as Bobby poured more coffee.

Manny judged the man to be about his own age. He was lanky and stood about five foot ten or eleven. A shock of dirty blond hair refused to be combed back from his high forehead. Mury had informed Manry the night before that Ned was a Leo, but although he had the shift looking cat's eyes that most Leo's did, Ned didn't have the snobbish air of "I'm King of the Jungle" that usually accompanied this sign.

Spearing a pancake from the pile, Manny broke the silence. "Well, you sound like you must be from Texas, Ned?"

"Fer sure, a long time ago," was the reply. Later, Manny was to observe that "fer sure" this response followed every phrase the man would utter.

As the two men ate, Manny wondered if Ned was also gay. He didn't appear to be, but Manny felt he was walking on eggs around this subject. Maybe Ned thought Manny was another of Mury's boyfriends.

Wanting to let Ned know where he stood sexually, Manny maneuvered the conversation around to the subject of women. Casually, Manny mentioned how much he liked women. This information seemed to put the shipper at ease, and he told Manny that he had an "old lady" out in San Jose.

"Even though I have my own place here in town, I spend most nights out there with my pretty Spanish lady. Her name's Maria."

"I'll have to meet her some time."

"Fer sure." Ned left the last pancake for Manny, excused himself, and disappeared through the back passageway.

As Bobby washed up the dishes, Manny lingered a while longer over his coffee. He contemplated his long trip west, his verbal and sexual battle with Mury, and finally decided that he would have to put everything out here aside so he could begin completing his book; a book which he hoped would help the world overcome the geological hurdles the cataclysms would bring.

A newspaper was lying on the table and Manny went to pick it up. No, he thought, I'd better concentrate on the book.

Had he picked up the paper and read it, he would have noticed that there were stories on the Mid East War and hints that the Arab nations were about to take the extreme step of cutting off all oil to the West, and that the comet Kohoutek was somewhere overhead being exalted by the world's scientists. Instead, Manny drained his cup, brushed his teeth, and made his way down the back stairs to Sourdough Sam's warehouse.

*   *   *

When he got downstairs Manny found the warehouse to be a beehive of activity. Someone had backed the rental to the side entrance of the building and several people were busy unloading the contents. Boxes were rolling down metal rollers, similar to those used back East at the State Hospital. As he moved closer, he found one of the workers was Mury. Manny nodded a greeting. As Manny approached, Mury stopped his work and said he wanted to introduce him to someone. Next to Mury stood a short man, thin but muscular and Manny noticed his quick smile and squinting eyes.

"Manny, I want you to meet Jerry Wilson, He runs the deli. He's also a Leo." Mury seemed to introduce everyone by their sun sign.

As Manny made small talk with Jerry, he felt that unlike Ned, this man did have the Leo "King of the Jungle" air of superiority about him. Something about the man gave Manny an immediate feeling distrust.

Next, Mury introduced Manny to two oriental boys. "I'd like you to meet the two best ping pong players I've ever seen." Manny shook their hands and mentally, christened them "Ping" and "Pong."

More introductions followed as Jerry signaled Ned to take his place on the unloading line and insisted that Manny meet Jerry's wife, Margo. Jerry led them out to the General Store explaining that was where Margo worked. Manny was surprised to find she was Chinese.

"What's your sign, Manny?" was Margo's first statement to him.

"I'm a Pisces." Manny announced.

"I can already tell you're a Pisces. I mean your rising and moon."

"I'm not sure what you mean, but if I find out you'll be the first to know." Manny was captivated by the woman's china doll charms and wondered what kind of relationship she and Jerry had. Maybe something could be worked out. All at once Jerry announced he had to leave and pick up their son, Abe, at school. Looking around Manny saw that Mury and left and only Margo and he were the only people left in the Deli. It was hard to read her age, but she was at least five foot six, tall for someone Chinese.

Her smile was captivating as she asked, "Well Manny how was your trip from the East?"

Manny explained the circumstances of the overloaded truck and the storm in the Sierras, but said that all in all it wasn't too bad. He mentioned that his head felt as if it were still on the highway, but quickly his English side jumped in with the stiff upper lip influence and added he would get over that soon.

Still mulling over the wild possibility of getting together with this captivating woman, Manny inquired about her sun sign which she told him was Sagittarius. Reluctant to leave, Manny asked if she was from San Francisco.

"No. Jerry and I are both from New York." She went on to explain how after they had married they had moved to Israel and lived on a kibbutz. Neither she nor Jerry had cared for Kibbutz life and after a year they moved back to New York and later to San Francisco. Eventually they had met Sourdough Sam and now they were part of the family.

As Manny listened to Margo talk he felt a very strong attraction to her. Ever since Vietnam Manny had felt one day he would meet an Oriental woman who would change his life. He thought maybe Margo was this woman.

Customers entered the Deli and Margo excused herself to wait on them.

Standing alone for a moment Manny suddenly heard the sound of rollers which pulled him back to the warehouse. Manny saw still another person had been added to the relay team unloading the rental. Mury soon introduced Manny to another member of the family, Randy.

Randy was good looking and dressed neatly. He was short and probably somewhere in his middle twenties. The most noticeable thing about him, other than his curly blond hair, was the pair of gloves he wore. As they shook hands Manny enquired about the gloves with thin holes across the knuckles.

Again, Manny remembered Mury mentioning Randy the night before. Apparently, Randy worked as a truck driver for Sourdough Sam's and was one of Sam's favorites he also came from the North East, Connecticut.

Manny remembered Mury had also said that the two men had met in the Army but that now Randy considered himself an actor. Manny had an odd feeling about this man which was intensified after Randy offered him a weak gloved handshake.

Soon Manny had been drawn into helping the others unload the truck. After a while the unloading became a game to everyone and soon it didn't even seem like work. People yelled and screamed, joked and laughed, and before Manny knew it Margo was asking everyone what they wanted for lunch.

Manny listened in awe to the strange and odd concoctions people wanted on their sandwiches. When his turn came he told Margo, "I don't go for anything fancy. Couldn't I just have a plain roast beef with mustard?"

"Aw, come on, Manny. Try something new. If you don't like it, you don't have to eat it."

"Okay," Manny relented. He couldn't resist her and would learn all his sign. He had to see if there really was any connection between him and this alluring lady.

During lunch, Manny told Mury about the unemployment checks he had been drawing back home. Mury said it was a simple procedure to have them sent directly to San Francisco. He suggested that Randy drive Manny to the local unemployment office after lunch so Manny could sign up.

* * *

The company car was a little red Hornet and as soon as Randy moved the car into traffic, Manny's head was zapped with another hum. He had hoped' to see some of the sights of the city, but his eyes were out of focus. Fast moving scenery and blurred people on the streets mixed with that constant hum. Manny rubbed his eyes and tried to clear his head.

Randy, being an actor, knew exactly where the unemployment office was located. It was obvious that Randy wasn't thrilled about driving the newcomer around, but he attempted to act as tour guide. Being in San Francisco, the talk turned to the subject of earthquakes.

Manny confided his fear of the city crumbling into the ocean. Immediately, Randy slammed on the brakes and pulled the car to the side of the road. Randy pulled a map and pencil from the glove compartment. He began to draw a thin line across the area he had heard was the most vulnerable to earthquakes. Manny noticed the line ran across a part of greater San Francisco called Daly City.

The way Randy handled the car and map, Manny felt he might be trying to feed Manny's fears. A few minutes later Randy restarted the car and dropped Manny off in front of the unemployment office and went to park the car. Once inside, Manny found the office was set up differently back home and it took a few minutes to get oriented. He saw a sign marked, NEW APPLICANTS, and joined the line. Long lines seemed to be something all unemployment offices had in common.

Half an hour later, Manny finally reached the woman at the counter, only to be told that he had to go to the OUT OF TOWN section. Manny wanted to ask why there wasn't a sign indicating this in the first place, but resigned himself to another long wait.

Forty minutes later Manny was interviewed by a pleasant middle-aged woman. After filling out several forms, the woman informed him that he would have to come back every other Monday to sign up. She said that he would receive his checks in the mail directly from his home state. She warned him not to expect them for at least ten weeks, and then added that in their previous experience with Massachusetts, it might be even longer. Thanking her, Manny made his way back to the car.

On the ride back to Sourdough Sam's Randy barely said a word. Manny didn't mind, everything looked even more blurry to Manny than before. Between his late night and the interruption of the driving hum in his head, he could hardly make out the signs they passed.

Suddenly Randy made a quick turn up a hill and stopped. He told Manny he had an errand but would be back shortly. The "shortly" turned into fifteen minutes. What's the difference, Manny thought to himself? As old Cheech and Chong would say, "I'm not into time mannn."

Another fifteen minutes passed, but Manny still didn't mind. The writer's weary blurred mind was a jumble of thoughts. What was happening back home; how were Susan and the kids; don't forget to write Miranda; Mury Nestor seemed okay; earthquakes.

The idea of earthquakes shook Manny from his thoughts. He glanced at a clock on the building across the street and figured he'd been sitting in the parked car for over an hour. Now he began to worry. What the hell could Randy be doing he thought? How could he leave me so long? Which house did he go into? It's getting late! On and on raced Manny's mind, until all at once the car door flew open.

"You all set to go?" Randy sounded as if Manny had only been waiting a few minutes. Well maybe he had. His only reply was a quick, "Yah."

*   *   *

It was late afternoon by the time the Hornet pulled up to Sourdough Sam's. The rental had been parked back across the street where Manny had left it the night before. As he and Randy entered the warehouse, they came upon a life and death ping pong match. Mury and Ned were on one team against the Oriental boys on the other. Jack was rolling a joint and between serves, Mury called to Manny to go upstairs and fix himself a drink.

Manny was taking a third hit from the joint when the game ended and he heard Ned utter a good natured, "We'll get you fer sure next time." Manny handed the joint to Ned, who declined saying he had to play a game with his "old lady." Someone mentioned that the ping pong game and joint were an after work ritual at Sourdough Sam's. Mury took the joint from Manny and joined the group.

After taking a hit of the join Mury handed the pot back to Manny and exclaimed. "Say you old Portagee, how'd you like to go out on the town with me tonight. Maybe a little dinner and then we can hit a few spots in North Beach. We better do it now, I read in News and World Report today that oil might be cut off and the presidents in trouble." What Mury didn't throw in was that Kohoutek was getting closer.

The stoned Manny barely heard him but he did answer after glancing at Ned. "Fer sure." It was catchy.

SEVEN

Later that same night, Manny and Mury were seated in a cab on their way to North Beach. Mury, acting as tour guide, had the cab driver take the long route in order to indicate points of interest. The two new friends got out on Grant Street and walked through several gay clubs.

It was obvious to Manny that Mury was showing him off, but he didn't mind. He knew he looked good and that made him feel good. Besides, after his battle with Mury the other night, he felt secure in his heterosexuality.

The energy flowing through San Francisco was beginning to affect him and he found himself relaxing. Every now and then the Portuguese side of him would ignite his natural defenses causing him to adopt an air of gruffness when they entered the homosexual establishments. At one well known gay restaurant, Manny's heterosexual tough guy routine was especially noticeable.

"What will it be gentlemen?" The waiter asked preparing to take down their orders.

"Steak, rare," was Manny's curt reply.

"Why don't you try the cheese soufflé, or the escargot? They're both quite good tonight."

"I don't like that kind of stuff," Manny replied in a rough construction worker voice.

"And you sir?" Puzzled the waiter turned to Mury.

"I'll have whatever the crazy Portagee' here is having."

"Is there anything else," again to Mury.

"We'll have a bottle of good red wine."

"I'll have a Grandad on the rocks." Manny broke in roughly, even though he loved wine with dinner.

Observing that Manny wasn't at all acting like his usual self, and sensing where some of his anxiety might be coming from, Mury brought up the subject of writing to try and relax his guest. "Listen here, Manny. As your manager," he dragged out the word manager, almost as a drawl. "I really believe things are starting to come together. Being in this place, I see another place," he used a strong emphasis on the word place. "In that place, I see a direction. Now, what you have to do as the writer is write. And what I have to do as manager is manage But first, we've got to find a place for you to work. Somewhere you can have privacy. Sourdough Sam's has too many distractions. I'll pay the rent and give you spending money when you need it. How does that sound, ol' buddy?" Manny said it sounded great to him and grunted thanks to the waiter when he brought his drink.

Trying again to draw Manny out, Mury asked if he liked the tube.

"Yes, I find that it can calm down my mind," Manny answered.

"That's right," Mury agreed affably. "You know what our good friend Marshall McLuhan says." Mury had a way of using a famous name as if the person were an actual friend.

"The media is the message. Now, what I say is, the media is the massage."

More conversation, then dinner, and finally home to do a 'bowl' and watch the tube.

*   *   *

After a Taxi dropped the two men off at Sourdough Sam's, Mury turned on the tube but they did more talking than watching.

Mury favored the educational stations. Even though the agreed, they compared KQED in San Francisco with WGBH in Boston. When the news came on, a running dialogue flew across the room between them as each news item was announced.

A picture of Nixon passed across the screen.

"Yaaaaaah, Manny," Mury always drew out his 'yaaaaaah's' for emphasis. If I were Nixon I'd say, look here Golda," here he stretched out the name Golda, "Look here, Anwar," another long stretch. "Either you two get your shit together or we are going to take your fucking oil and take your fucking kibbutz's and make peanut butter out of them."

"But you can't do that!" Manny nearly flew across the room in excited exasperation.

Who says we can't. All we have to do is do it! If we're supposed to be the strongest country in the world, why do we have to take shit from these piss whole countries? What good is it to have all the muscle if you can't use it?"

The question hung poised in the air. After a moment Manny retrieved it in an attempt at calmness. "You would have liked a paper I wrote on Vietnam for a class in Problems of Democracy back in '64." I felt, at least at the time, I felt this that we should end the Vietnam War militarily, and if China stepped in to interfere we should bomb them immediately rather than wait for them to build a nuclear capability. It was a well written paper."

"What grade did you get on it?"

"B, or maybe B plus, I don't remember. The teacher didn't agree with all that I said. The protestors were already coming alive and she leaned in their direction."

Mury posed another question. "Did you get an ID bracelet with a POW's name on it?" His sarcastic tone left little doubt how he felt about the subject.

"No," Manny replied laughing. "I felt that most of the POW's were flyers. They did tour after tour because combat missions were worth good money. I felt they should be expected to answer for their actions if they were shot down. Besides, I'm convinced that if a POW knew that some commie pinko college kid was running around wearing a bracelet with his name on it, he'd rather be dead."

Manny paused for a moment and said in a more serious tone, "I know it sounds cold, but the people of the United States had to lose those forty or fifty thousand people to learn they couldn't be the policemen of the world. After all, if you look back, there were protests in World War II, and more in the Korean War; the whole thing simply built to a crescendo in Vietnam."

"Yes, you're right," Mury agreed, "but the top government officials didn't give a damn about those people they lost. After all, they were only working class kids and "niggers."

The manager and the writer were really cooking now. Discussion followed discussion and sometimes they were heated and intense. Sparks seemed to fly between the two as they went through such subjects as culture, politics, parapsychology, sociology and philosophy.

"Listen Manny, even if Nixon did send out the plumbers, look at all he's doing in foreign policy. At least he had us talking to Russia and China."

Manny answered in a rush of excitement that made his voice jump an octave so it squeaked. "He only did that to get himself re-elected. The only thing that guy knows how to do is run for office. If he could stop the war in his second term, why couldn't he do it in his first one?

He doesn't know what the hell to do now because there's no other office to go after. Nixon is a direct result of the educational system in this country. It doesn't matter how you get an 'A', as long as you get it; Watergate proved that. To Nixon, an election is the same as getting an 'A' in school. It doesn't matter if you cheat, as long as you get the 'A'. That's why this country is so fucked up; that's why we need those cataclysms, so the system can be knocked down and rebuilt!"

"How many people do you think will survive?"

"I've heard estimates as high as ten percent of the population to as low as one hundred and forty-four thousand people.

According to Edgar Cayce, many people who died during the fall of Atlantis were reincarnated starting after the end of World War II. They've been sent here because they've lived through mass destructions before and now they can help people after the cataclysms." Manny paused for a moment and added, "Possibly that's who you and I are."

"Praise the Lord and pass the peanut butter," Mury replied, and then in a much more serious vein, "I feel strongly that we are the people to do it."

Listening to Mury, Manny felt as if the man's words were coming from the mouth of a mystic seeing into the future.

For a moment Mury was silent and then he leaned closer to Manny. "I'm going to let you in on a special deal, but it would be premature to go into the details right now." An odd feeling crept through Manny, but he kept his mouth shut.

As the evening came to a close, Mury insisted on reading Manny's palm. Each prediction was made as if it were gospel. At the end of the reading Mury told Manny that although he would be successful in his writing endeavors, he would never attain the fame and recognition he desired.

"Well Manny, it's time this silly girl got her beauty rest." He stood up, stretched and yawning loudly headed for the bedroom.

Manny called to him, "I'm staying up to watch a little more tube. Do you have an extra blanket and pillow? Think I'll sleep on the couch tonight."

"Suit yourself you old Portagee' turd." They both laughed.

As Manny lay watching the television his mind recalled all the events that had transpired since he arrived in San Francisco. Things were certainly different than he'd expected. He liked Mury. He felt the two of them thought very much alike and shared many common beliefs. It was a nice feeling. As long as Mury respected his heterosexuality and didn't hassle him, they could have a good working relationship.

Manny suppressed a yawn. He was tired and it felt good. San Francisco felt good, too. He wondered if people back home, Susan or Miranda would believe him when he told them about Sourdough Sam's. He'd never worked for a place like that before. Manny wondered about his own behavior. He certainly wasn't himself. He felt changed but he wasn't exactly sure how or why. He covered himself with the blanket Mury had thrown him. Mury, he felt Mury was a friend.

It occurred to him that it had been a long time since he'd had a male friend. He switched off the television and closed his eyes. It was a nice feeling.

*   *   *

Bright sunlight pouring through the window woke Manny the next morning. He thought a moment and remembered it was Saturday. All of a sudden he felt the pain; the side of his jaw was on fire. It couldn't be a toothache because the pain went all the way up to his eye.

"I need coffee and then aspirin, lots of aspirin," he thought. Two cups of coffee and three aspirins later and his jaw was still inflamed. Looking out the window Manny noticed people were walking around in shorts. He checked the thermometer and saw that it registered sixty degrees.

"How come I'm freezing?" he asked no one in particular.

Mury and Bobby suggested huge doses of vitamin E and C; their remedy for any and all ailments.

"I don't believe in vitamins," Manny protested. "If you take too many of them your body stops producing them naturally. Then what do you do if a cataclysm comes along and you can't get any vitamins."

"Don't worry about it," Mury replied, "I'm working on a deal to buy a pharmaceutical distributorship. We'll have enough vitamins to last a lifetime."

"What the hell!" Manny took the pills.

Bobby suggested meditation but Manny was in too much pain to concentrate. Finally, he announced he was going for a walk.

"Okay," Mury replied, "but don't forget we have to return the rental today or we have to pay extra.

Walking up Thirtieth, Manny turned right at Geary. The area was beautiful. The architecture had a Spanish flavor, and the homes were new looking with gardens in front. The whole area inspired the fledgling young writer. He remembered Mury telling him this area was called the Sunset District. He tried to concentrate on the beauty surrounding him, but a pain shot through his jaw. He tried to distract himself with memories of home but his whole face was suffused with pain, as an agonizing ache shot up his left jaw.

Reaching the top of the hill Manny saw the Pacific Ocean. He was flooded with feeling. "The Pacific Ocean!" From coast to coast! From sea to shining sea. I made it. I'm a writer. I know I'm going to make it big."

He noticed a building to his right called the "Cliff House" and vowed to come back and have a drink there some time. Standing on top of the hill he watched the seals swimming and heard them barking. "Seals" he thought, "if only my jaw would stop hurting."

It had been several hours since his last aspirin and now it would be fine to take more. Quickly he reversed his course and headed for Sam's, but he could hardly walk the pain was so intense. He took his first left and seeing a sign reading Clement Street, took a right. Soon he saw the SAVEMORE store and knew he should be just a few blocks from Sourdough Sam's.

Another pain shot through him. What can be causing this pain in my face?" he thought.

He remembered his Saturday headaches: terrible headaches he used to get every Saturday since his return from Vietnam. The pain in his jaw was almost as bad as the pain from those headaches. They had become so bad sometimes he was disabled for several days at a time.

Tears began streaming down his face. The pain was becoming excruciating and Manny wanted to scream but then people would know he was crying. He couldn't let anyone see the tears; he wouldn't even let himself wince in the dentist's chair. The tears made him angry; angry at the pain itself.

"Stop it," he commanded himself. "You can't do anything about the pain so you might as well relax and let it happen." He allowed himself to feel the pain; he went right to the very center of its existence. He could feel lines of pain stretching across his left jaw from his lower molars to his chin.

As he walked down the white cement sidewalk towards Sourdough Sam's he could feel the pain travel up through his nose and into his cheekbone. He felt the pain, and then all of a sudden it was gone. Amazed, Manny stopped dead in his tracks. He waited for the pain to streak through his jaw once more, but nothing happened. He turned his head from side to side and probed his chin and still nothing happened.

"I did it. I cured the pain myself!" he exclaimed to Clement Street and the world. "Maybe San Francisco is the place for me. Maybe this is a magic rock."

Suddenly thoughts of Miranda flooded into his head. He wanted to tell someone who knew him well, someone who would understand how he felt. Someone who wouldn't think he was crazy.

Entering the side door to Sourdough Sam's, Manny said a quick hello to Ned and headed straight for the typewriter in Mury's office. He didn't know what he wanted to say or exactly where to begin. There were so many things that had happened to him in the past week and a half, so many new discoveries and feelings.

The typewriter was electric and Manny hadn't used one since high school. He put his fingers on the keys and tried to let his thoughts flow:

Manuel H Sounds

The quick brown fox jumped over the lazy dog. How do you do. I am fine today how are you. I am fine lets go now. do it. it can be very fun and easy. Let me see now am I ready to write a letter to Miranda. The trip is really far out, but it is so far out that it is in. Everything is working out, some of it as I expected and some that I didn't. Even the immense pain I've already felt since I've been here has helped me grow. I love you, darling, and I'm fighting very hard not to feel it yet. I've realized that I'm not Superman but I can help create one out of Man. I'm safe here and its all I can write for now, to many of the feelings start to creep in,

Manny

Manny sat back and stared at the words in front of him. Writing had unleashed his feelings of sadness and longing. Longing for his kids and Susan; for his house and friends. Trying to distract his mind and numb the feelings, he found a Sourdough Sam envelope and had Ned run it through the stamp meter. Dropping the letter in the OUT box he headed towards the delicatessen. He wanted to find the pretty Chinese lady Margo and tell her about the healing experience.

The afternoon slipped by quickly. Ned had located a rental company where they could return the truck, and the two men set off together. On the way home their conversation turned to women. Manny told Ned he was a lifelong heterosexual and felt it was time he got out to meet some San Francisco ladies. Ned rubber stamped the idea with his usual, 'Fer Sure.'

Back at the shop Manny found Mury and told him he had received one hundred and seventy-five dollars back from the deposit on the truck. Mury told him to keep the money. Including the fifty dollars Manny had left over from the trip cross country, Manny now had two hundred and thirty dollars. "Not bad," he thought to himself, "considering all I had when I left home was a little change."

Later that night the writer and his new manager went to dinner at Victoria Station. They were both in good moods, whooping, singing, and as usual talking of ways to solve the problems of the world. They were building a solid relationship, and each man felt they finally had found someone who could keep up with their high levels of energy and also had some of the same philosophical ideas.

Back at Mury's apartment the conversation eventually turned to Manny's writing. Manny asked how soon Mury wanted him to begin, and exactly what publishing plans he had in mind. Mury told him he would hire someone to edit and all Manny had to do was knock it out.

"Leave all the rest of it to me; I'm your manager now."

Mury was full of plans and they included more than just publishing a book. Manny sat in amazement as he listened to the man outline some of the projects he was working on or planning to work on: a deal with Pillsbury to sell sourdough pancake mix in conjunction with Bundt Pans; an expansion of the imported tea business that was doing so well; a possible franchise of Sourdough Sam's General Stores; subsidizing a consulting business that Mury's father was interested in starting; researching a strange energy machine that Margo's uncle was working on, which she had assured Mury, was almost ready to be patented.

"All I need is some extra 'cash. Cash that the government won't know about."

The talk was light and fun that night until all at once Mury became very serious.

"You know that deal I mentioned to you?" Manny nodded and the smile disappeared from his face. He had that odd feeling again.

"Well, it might be going down sooner than I planned. Do you know anyone on the east coast who might be able to get rid of a large quantity of cocaine?"

Strangely enough, the words hit Manny as if they were a natural extension of their philosophical and political discussions. He felt no shock. He hesitated for a moment trying to find the best answer to Mury's question.

Was there anyone I knew? He re-phrased the question in his mind. The answer came quickly. Yes, he thought, my cousin who visited me just before I left for San Francisco, Al Silva.

"Well?" Mury was waiting for an answer.

"As a matter of fact, I might. I know someone who's into a lot of heavy stuff. He might even have connections with the Irish Mafia, Whitey Bolger's gang."

Mury's reply was quick and to the point. "You're willing to try and set up a deal?"

"Why not," Manny's reply was just as quick.

"If it will help the Sourdough Family, I'll do it." The two men shook hands and embraced. Finally Mury broke away.

"I can't tell you any of the details yet, but it will be happening soon. Now, I'm going to mix you one of my special Compari cocktails and we'll drink to the future and turds."

*　　*　　*

The next morning Manny woke craving bacon and eggs. Not finding any in the refrigerator he looked out the window to check the weather. It looked like a nice day so he decided to take a stroll to the SAVEMORE and buy some.

He was just turning into the front entrance to Sourdough Sam's with his bag of groceries when Margo and Jerry pulled up in their '53 Hudson. Walking over to the car to say hello, Manny noticed that besides their son, there was a fourth person in the car. As the stranger emerged from the back seat, Manny was introduced by Margo.

"Manny, this is Rocket." Manny stared at the man for a moment. He was an enormous hulk of a man with a thick 'Fu Manchu' moustache. He wore a green army fatigue jacket and on his head was an old and worn cowboy hat.

"Hi" Manny found his voice.

Not bothering to answer the hello, Rocket ordered Manny to inform Mury that he had arrived. "Tell him I'm going to have a few words with Margo and Jerry and then I'll be up."

"Sure," Manny replied to the surly request and continued on his way. Manny found Mury making coffee in the kitchen. Setting his groceries on the counter he turned to Mury. "There's a man here to see you about the cocaine deal." Manny had no idea where the words came from; they simply jumped out of his mouth.

"Who is it?" Mury didn't miss a beat.

"Margo says his name is Rocket."

"Okay, then. When he comes in, let me do the talking. I don't want him to know anything about you yet."

Suddenly Manny had a flash. "Listen Mury. I still have a bunch of CHARLES T. SHORT business cards from that movie I told you about. Why don't you introduce me as Charles?"

"Fantastic idea. I'll take him out on the patio and start talking bus_ness. You stay in here and finish the coffee, or breakfast, or whatever, and then come out and slowly work your way into the conversation."

"Sounds good to me."

Mury went out to set up the lounge chairs and table while Manny busied himself in the kitchen. It wasn't long before Manny heard heavy footsteps on the porch which connected Mury's apartment with Sourdough Sam's where Jerry and Margo had been staying in Sam's absence. He heard a knock and then Mury's footsteps as he went to answer the door. The greeting that followed was unlike any Manny had seen. The two men embraced and even, kissed. It sounded like a reunion between two long lost soul mates. Manny expected to see tears streaming down their faces. Hugging and patting each other, the two walked through the kitchen and out onto the patio. Manny asked if he'd like coffee. As Rocket passed him, Manny took his grunt to mean yes.

Manny puttered around the kitchen until Mury poked his head in and asked if the coffee was ready yet. Placing the cups and cream and sugar on a tray, Manny made his way out to the patio. Setting the tray on the table, Manny could sense that Rocket had changed his attitude about him. Now, he behaved cordially, almost in a friendly manner.

He even called Manny his little brother.

Taking his coffee, Manny pulled up a chair across from the two men. They were discussing jewelry. Apparently Rocket and his old lady ran a jewelry shop in Mendocino, and Rocket had brought some samples.

Mury was looking through them and stopped as one in particular caught his eye. Rocket explained that it was a magic ring and worth seventy-five dollars. As Mury handled the ring, turning it over and over, Manny noticed it was indeed beautiful. It was a silver ring with a stone of agate the size of a nickel. Embedded in the agate was what Rocket said was fossilized black algae. The algae took the exact shape of the tree of life. Mury handed the ring to Manny.

"It's for you." Manny tried it on. It fit perfectly.

As Rocket rolled a joint, Mury caught Manny's eye. "Rocket here, says he would like to do a cocaine deal with us."

"Oh, yah? What does he have in mind?" Manny tried to sound aloof and casual, as if he did this every day, but being sure to adopt the heavy voice of a Hollywood gangster.

Mury jumped in playing the straight man, "Why don't you explain your plan, Rocket?"

The big man lit the joint, took a long hit and passed it to Mury. As he exhaled a long stream of smoke, he began to spin his tale.

"Well, ya' see, I've been a poor boy all my life. I never had a chance to get any education. I can't even read or write. I've always been a loser, but I know I could make it if only I could get one good break." He leaned back and took another hit off the joint

Watching him, Manny felt that 'all his life' could have been forty or even fifty years. The man's weather beaten face made it hard to guess his age.

Exhaling another stream of smoke, Rocket picked up his story. "All I want is to be able to buy me a good sail boat and take my old lady on a cruise around the world. I know I can do it. My time is here. I have these connections in Columbia where I can get me all the cocaine I can handle. All I need is someone to front the operation and everyone gets rich."

Manny broke in gruffly. "How do you plan to get the cocaine into the country?"

"That's the best part." Rocket was getting more and more excited. "I have this friend who has this plastic stuff that looks just like human skin. What I plan to do is; take six people through a crash course in karate and parachute jumpin', then have each lose enough weight to be five pounds under passport weight, then leave Columbia with five pounds of cocaine stuffed into the plastic stuff, which we shape onto our backs so it looks like our spines. Then, each one of us takes a different route back into the country." Rocket sat back and finished the last of the joint.

Manny didn't laugh, he didn't even snicker. He was taking this man seriously. A small voice in the back of his mind told him he should tell the guy the plan was crazy and catch the first plane back to Massachusetts. Of course, he didn't. Instead, he felt compelled to push one step further with the whole scheme. Of course he knew damn well he wasn't going to take karate lessons, nor was he going to jump out of any plane, but he also knew that if a reasonable plan could be found, he was going through with the deal. After all, with the money Sourdough Sam's could publish his book; with the book published maybe the world could be saved.

Manny glanced up at Rocket and noticed that Mury, too, was watching the man. Simultaneously the two turned towards each other and as if reading each other's thoughts, then shook their heads. The unspoken message was clear. "It doesn't look good." All at once Mury broke the silence and began listing the objections.

"In the first place, Rocket, I can't leave Sourdough Sam's right now. Secondly, Manny's family would never go for an idea like that. Other than the obvious danger to him physically, if he were ever caught the family might be implicated and that would mean serious repercussions up and down the entire East Coast."

Rocket looked up in surprise. "Who's his family?"

As if on cue, Manny produced one of his CHARLES T. SHORT business cards, and handed it to Rocket. Looking confused, Rocket asked, "What's this production company thing?"

Mury jumped in acting as spokesman. "The film company is only a front for a mafia organization. Manny here, well, I think you can draw your own conclusions. The point is the organization is hot to do a cocaine deal, but they wouldn't be too happy if a family member got hurt."

Rocket just looked at Manny.

Mury continued, "The thing is, this has to be a one man, one shot deal. We'll front the money for the trip and the cocaine, but you have to do it yourself."

"Alright, I can do it." Rocket returned Mury's level stare. The two men remained locked that way until Manny broke the tension.

"There's one more thing, Rocket."

"What's that?" Rocket shifted his gaze to Manny.

Once again the words appeared from nowhere. If anything goes wrong, you'll be killed."

EIGHT

The three men smoked another joint and talked until Rocket suggested that the trio snort some cocaine to seal their agreement. Retiring to the living room, Mury produced a mirror and razor while Rocket took a packet of cocaine from his shirt pocket.

"Ssssss ..... nnnn…ifff….ssssii …iffffffff.Sssss ... nnniiiiii.. fff."

Soon the subject of women came up. Rocket felt that the most beautiful women in the world lived in San Francisco. Mury merely grunted, and Manny commented that he hadn't had a chance to find out yet. This prompted Mury to suggest that since he himself wasn't partial to women, maybe Rocket would take Manny out on the town to remedy the situation. The idea seemed to appeal to Rocket and while he and Murray had joint for the road, Manny changed into some partying clothes.

The transportation for the expedition was to be Rocket's Olympia Beer truck. The truck looked as worn and beaten as the man who drove it. Not only was the cab filthy and full of garbage, but the tip of the cargo box was smashed in as if it hadn't made it under a low bridge. However, like Rocket himself, the old truck had plenty of power. Rocket pointed out the truck had a 409 cubic-inch engine and then started the engine with a roar. Rocket put his baby through her paces and the two new business partners tore across San Francisco headed for their first drink.

It wasn't long before Manny understood why this crazy man was called Rocket. Not only was he a double Gemini, but he was filled with so much energy it seemed as if he were ready for take-off at any second. During their visit to the first bar, Manny watched in awe as Rocket proceeded to balance five straws on his bulbous nose, balance a weighted bar table on his chin, and after requesting a butcher knife from the bartender, balance the razor sharp point on the tip of first his nose, his chin, and finally, his ear lobe. The bartender poured both men drinks after the last feat.

Rocket repeated his repertoire in the second bar, and by the time they arrived at the third bar, was so proficient in his act that he attracted a crowd of people around their table. As Manny and the crowd stood ready to watch his next trick, Rocket suddenly slammed his briefcase down on the table, flipped open the lid and began hawking his jewelry. As the crowd quickly dispersed, Manny asked the man where he had learned such tricks. Rocket replied that he had worked for several years as a strong man in a circus.

The two men ordered more drinks and talked. Manny mentioned he was writing a book. Rocket told him he wished he could put his thoughts on paper because he always felt his life story would make a great book.

Questioning him further, Manny learned that Rocket had been born the youngest of twin boys to a somewhat affluent family. When he was seven years old the family had taken a steamer around the globe, when Rocket, clowning as usual, had fallen overboard. He managed to grab a piece of wood floating in the water. Rocket stayed afloat until the current swept him ashore somewhere along the western coast of Africa.

After a few days of wandering through the strange land, Rocket was captured by a huge black warrior and carried by the man for seven days and nights through the sweltering jungle. He stayed with a tribe of natives until he made his escape eight years later at the age of fifteen. He told Manny this was the reason he never learned to read or write. After his escape, he made his way to Europe where he teamed up with a circus. Due to his strength and large size, he became a strongman and was given a set of barbells and a leopard skin loincloth. He also grew a handlebar moustache. Rocket continued spinning yarn after yarn until Manny suggested they head for another bar on Union Street.

Sitting at a horse-shoe shaped bar in a place called Slater Hawkins, Manny and Rocket saw their first female prospects of the day. One woman was rather tall with a large bone structure. She had strawberry blonde hair and while attractive enough, wasn't super beautiful. The other woman had auburn colored hair and flashing eyes with a smile to match. They had ordered drinks and were talking quietly together at the other end of the bar, when Rocket leaned over and asked them if they liked jewelry. Naturally, they did, especially since the dark haired lady was wearing a beautiful turquoise necklace. Rocket invited them to join him for drinks at a table and went out to the truck to get his briefcase.

Steering them to the table, Manny introduced himself. The tall woman did the talking for both women. She introduced herself as Gail, and said her friend's name was Iris.

Manny, adopting the role of a Mafia Don, ordered drinks for everyone. Soon Rocket returned with his wares and started into his act. First he lit a cigarette, and then with a flick of his finger, popped it into his mouth. Next he balanced a table and chair on his chin. Using an accent that sounded like a cross between Wallace Beery and Long John Silver, he spun story after story. Finally he asked the bartender for a butcher knife, and when the man said he couldn't accommodate him, snapped open his briefcase and tried to sell the guy some jewelry.

Manny ordered another round of drinks and started a heavy head discussion with the woman who called herself Gail. As he and Gail chatted, he could hear an occasional 'Ah, me proud beauty,' as Rocket engaged Iris in conversation. Manny and Gail hit it off as though they had known each other all their lives.

Gail told him she was an Aries but didn't have some of the 'babyish' Aries traits because of her rising sign. Manny told her he was a Pisces and acted exactly like those Linda Goodman described in her book, 'Sun Signs.' The talk of astrology soon led to Edgar Cayce.

Relating Cayce's predictions about the forthcoming cataclysms to Gail, Manny found she was someone who shared his interests. Soon she invited him to go with her to see Betty Bathard at the Inner Light Center. She told Manny Betty was a psychic who did life readings just like Cayce. The conversation was just starting in on electromagnetic energy forces and the Oneness of the universe when it happened.

Suddenly Manny couldn't talk. He felt as if a magnetic force had grabbed him; forces that actually took hold of his head and made it turn toward Iris. The two looked at each other but didn't speak. Turning back to Gail, Manny said, "I'm sorry. I know you and I are probably perfect for each other, but something is pulling me to your friend."

Gail said she understood and Manny should go ahead and do his thing. However, she also gave him a warning. "Be careful of Iris, she can be tough on men."

Manny barely heard Gail's words as he turned to Iris. Soon the two were in deep conversation. Manny wanted to know everything about this woman who said she was thirty- three but looked twenty-three. Iris obliged. She told him she had left her father's ranch in North Dakota when she was seventeen to see the world. She had lived and worked in most of the major cities of the country and had been a stewardess for World Airlines and carried troops back and forth to Vietnam during the same period of time that Manny had served there.

She told him that she had gone back to Vietnam later, but not as a "doughnut dolly" as she called them, but in order to see the country.

The more Manny listened to this fascinating woman, the more he was intrigued. He listened as she told of hitchhiking through the Mid-East during the Arab Israel War in '67 and how she had taken a job in business as a medical equipment salesperson. She was forced to sue the company she worked for under the new equal rights laws and had won her case. Presently she was working as a saleswoman for another company but was attending law school at night. By the time Iris had finished the story of her life, Manny knew Iris was the woman for him. It was love at first sight. His search for a San Francisco lady had ended on the very night it began.

NINE

Charles T Short, alias, Manny Silva, ordered more drinks and chateaubriand for four. A group discussion was begun. It seemed that Gail's roommate, a Libran, was giving her a hard time about the rent and there were some accusations of stolen money. Iris, another Libran was lending moral and because she was studying law, legal support. Gail said her roommate was a Libra and Manny said he found it hard to believe a Libran could be so unfair. Gail and Iris thought if Manny felt that way he should go with them after dinner to Gail's apartment to look into the business myself. Rocket was asked along also but said he had other business. Getting Manny aside he whispered that his job was done now that he had helped me find these two fine beauties.

Sitting in the back of Iris's little blue VW on the way to Gail's Manny explained that writing was the reason I came to San Francisco. He said everything was going fine except for the fact that the man who was going to publish my book was gay and he wanted to get into his pants. He then related the story of his first night in town. Both of them felt he should look for another place to stay. As a matter of fact, Gail was going out of town to see her family at Thanksgiving and Manny was welcome to stay at her place the four of five days she was gone. He thanked her and said he would think about it.

When we got to Gail's her roommate was out. Another girl who was staying in the apartment said she had gone out with her boyfriend and would not be back that evening. Not being able to do anything about the problem, Manny suggested we call it a day. He was free to spend the night on Mury's couch or perhaps Iris could take him out to Daly City and lend him a sleeping bag. Manny also jumped in with the fact that he would like to see more of the city so the ride with Iris sounded like a good idea.

On the way to her place, Iris explained that when she had worked in the medical equipment sales company she had lived in a beautiful apartment owned by two gay guys up on Knob Hill. Then, even when she left that job after she had been in a car accident and insurance payment had helped her stay on the Hill a couple more years. When the payments ran out she decided that big business and the capitalist way of life was a lot of bullshit. She moved to Daly City to go back to school and live with the people. The people in her neighborhood being mostly from the Philippines.

Most of the ride was a blur of conversation. We got off the highway and she pointed out to Manny where he could catch BART, the train system, back to San Francisco in the morning. The next thing he knew, they were driving into her garage under the apartment complex. They climbed the three flights of open stairs up to her landing which was covered with arrangements of flowers and driftwood. She said she got most of it on a nearby beach where she does much of her studying.

It took two keys to open the door. Iris was afraid of break-ins. Her storage locker in the garage had already been broken into several times. With a click the door finally opened. The two walked into a tiny hall with a telephone sitting on a book case. Manny only had to turn his head to see in all four rooms of the apartment. Kitchen stood to his immediate right, living room front right, next to her kitchen. On his left was the bathroom and straight past that was the bedroom. She led Manny, to my disappointment, into the living room.

It was a medium size room with a picture window that looked across the roof of the next apartment building. Because it was on a hill, a good deal of Daly City could be seen, including some of the highway and hills on the other side of town. From Iris's, the houses strung along the hills looked like toys. Under the window was a carved wooden chest. Iris said she had gotten it on a trip to Java. To the right of the chest was an orange armchair along with a table and lamp. In the middle of the floor was a black bear skin rug with a black steamer trunk on top of it. On the trunk were a centerpiece, ash tray, and a roach clip. On either side of the trunk was a long sheepskin. Against the wall were pillows to sit on. On the opposite side of the room from the pillows was a wooden cabinet where she took some records to put on the stereo which was to the left of a closet she had hung their coats. On the wall opposite the window and behind where Manny stood was a stuffed chair and fern plant bigger than Mury's creeping Charley. On the wall were several pictures, but the one which caught my eye the most was a sectioned Japanese print which was over their heads when they sat on the pillows to do a doobie which was Iris' name for a joint.

Manny watched the smoke curl around Iris' pretty face as she put the last of the doobie on the roach clip. The clip part was like any other Manny had seen, but the handle was made of an indented Indian head nickel. When he held it, his thumb fit comfortably into the indentation. She said it had been a present from a man named Grant. He was a bastard and the last man she had been in love with except someone named Harvey who had worked with her at the medical supply company. She said, he really didn't count though because he was married. Besides, he had adopted a son and wouldn't leave his wife because of it. At any rate, this bastard Grant had given her the clip and it was the only thing of his left in the apartment. She said when an affair ends, it ends. "I throw out or return everything I ever got from the man and close him out of my life." She said the same goes for bad lovers. She had once told this guy who was a 'lousy Lay' that he was a 'lousy lay,' and to get out of her apartment and never come back.

It was Manny's turn now. He went through the whole gamete of women he had been to bed with in the last couple of years. He told her he was separated with two kids and had had many affairs with married women. To be sympathetic Manny told her he thought the single people in those type relationships are usually the ones who got hurt.

They did another doobie and talked for another hour before Iris stood up to announce bedtime. With a sly little smile on his face Manny stated that was fine with him. "Where can I sleep?" She said he could sleep in her bed as she liked to have someone to sleep with. But, there was to be no, she repeated, no fooling around. Manny said he thought it would be uncomfortable to sleep with her and not do anything as he was really turned on by her. She said in that case, he could sleep in her sleeping bag on the floor next to the bed.

In her room she stripped down to the buff. "Naturally," she said, "I always sleep in the nude." Her body looked like it got a lot of exercise. From her thighs up she was a picture pin-up girl. The only reason her whole body wasn't perfect was because she seemed to be standing on a pair of legs that belonged to someone else. It wasn't that they were ugly or anything, it was only that they didn't appear to belong to the rest of her. Her rear end, abdomen and breasts could have been sculptured by Michael Angelo. They were beautiful and he told her so. She took it as common knowledge and said something like, "naturally."

Manny stretched out on the bag and tried to wipe her out of his mind. He wasn't super horny even though she did attract him. It was something else. He couldn't put my finger on it. After rolling around he heard Iris ask him again to sleep with her. She really didn't like to sleep alone. Ah ha, here's my chance he thought. Manny slowly got off the floor and slipped under the sheets next to Iris.

He lay there a minute or two trying to decide if he should try anything or not. She had invited him into her bed, but her voice had been cold. It was more like a business proposition than an invitation to make love. He decided to try anyway. She was lying with her back to him and her knees drawn up. Manny was on his left side facing her back. He ran my left hand up her thigh, across the cheek, all over her hip and around to her stomach. He couldn't go any further. He pulled my hand back quickly. She was like a rock. Every muscle in her body was like piano wire. She made no attempt to turn towards him or give him any indication she wanted to continue. Manny tuned over, attempting to sleep.

TEN

Early Monday morning Iris dropped Manny at the BART station. The fast train whisked him into the city in no time and deposited him at the junction of Market and Powell. Manny couldn't believe the high levels of energy which surged into his feet and coursed through his entire body. As he took in the open-air flower markets, cable cars, and masses of elegantly dressed people, he felt as if he were sailing three feet off the ground. Only in Hong Kong, where he spent his R&R from Vietnam, had he seen such fashion conscious people. By the time he found his way to Sourdough Sam's it was already time for the lunch sandwich orders. Slipping in the side entrance, he was greeted to a friendly chorus of 'Where have you been?' and 'How's it going?'

Everyone was busy working. Ned was labeling jars and Mury was busy writing checks. Bobby introduced him to a carpenter with a Jesus-like beard who was installing a new counter between the deli and workshop and to a girl he'd never seen before named Edna, who was busy assembling breadmaking kits. Ignoring the insinuations Mury made about his whereabouts last night, Manny headed straight to the deli to tell Margo about the new Libran he had met.

He was still talking about Iris later that afternoon when he drove with Randy over to the 'Cannery' to deliver some tea to a specialty shop run by a friend of Mury's. On the return trip Manny suddenly felt a flash in his body which told him to call Iris immediately. He told Randy to pull over at the first pay phone he saw and dialed her number. The phone rang several times before Iris answered.

"Hello, this is Iris Ivory," she answered in a business-like voice.

"Oh, hi." She didn't sound too enthused to hear from him.

"Listen, there's something I have to tell you."

"What." Still no enthusiasm, maybe even less.

"I want to move in with you." The words came out in a rush of excitement.

"Well, I don't know if that's such a good idea."

"Can't we at least get together to talk about it. There's something else I have to talk to you about, too. It's about this deal I'm getting involved in with this guy Mury. The one I told you about."

"You mean the homo who runs the Sourdough place?"

"Yes."

"Alright. I'll meet you tonight at Perry's. It's down the street from the bar we met at."

"Great. I'll see you about nine."

Hesitating, Iris finally said, "No. Make it eleven. I have a few things to do."

"Okay, but don't forget to think about us living together. With all the craziness going on, I know it would be just perfect."

"We'll see. Bye." She hung up before he could get out his goodbye.

As Randy drove back to Sam's, Manny was full of anticipation about tonight's meeting with Iris. It never occurred to him to question his sudden impulse in asking a woman he barely knew, and hadn't even made love to, if he could move in with her. He was also totally oblivious to the huge ice crystal comet Kohoutek moving across the sky. What he did know was that he had to have this woman. H could hardly wait to tell her about the upcoming dope deal. He felt sure she was the type of person who would consider it an adventure. Besides, Sourdough Sam's could use a few more women around the place.

The day passed slowly for the lovesick Pisces. He couldn't wait to see Iris again and no amount of distraction helped. No matter who he was talking to he kept seeing her auburn hair, brown eyes and perfect bright smile.

By nine o'clock, Manny was showered, dressed and waiting impatiently for the time to pass so Randy could drive him to the appointed place to meet his new love. He was restlessly pacing while Mury and Randy passed a joint back and forth listening to Mury recording of Yaoundé Menuhin meets Ravi Shankar when the telephone rang. Passing Manny the joint, Mury answered it. "It's for the ugly Portagee'. It sounds like a woman."

Manny wondered who it could be.

"Hello, Manny. This is Iris Ivory."

"Hi"

"I'm sorry, but something terribly important has come up. I won't be able to make it tonight."

Hardly able to control the pain he felt, Manny answered. "You can't? Well . . . how about tomorrow night? There's something important I have to talk over with you."

"Tomorrow night. Tuesday . . . I don't know. I guess so. I'll meet you at the same place, same time."

"Good. See you then." Manny's mind was blank as he hung up the phone and walked back to the living room.

"What's the matter?" Mury asked.

"She isn't meeting me." All at once it began. Tears began to fill his eyes and the man who wouldn't allow himself to wince at the dentist's drill began sobbing into Mury's shoulder like a kid whose puppy had been run over by a car. Never before had Manny allowed a man to see his inner feelings, but he simply couldn't help himself.

Mury tried to console him and at the same time reassure Randy who was looking at Manny as if he was some weakling who'd gone off his rocker.

"Only a true author could feel such emotions."

Finally Manny calmed down enough to tell Mury that Iris couldn't meet him tonight and had postponed the meeting.

"Until when?"

"Until tomorrow night." Manny replied.

"That's only twenty-hour hours."

"Twenty-four hours . . . yah . . . that's not so long." Suddenly Manny felt better.

The three men passed the rest of the evening having drinks and listening to music and talking. Soon, the subject of women was introduced. Mury began talking about what ball busters women were. Manny, thinking he meant Iris, began to get defensive. One thing led to another and soon there was a heated argument.

"You only wish you were as sensitive as women." Manny was shouting at the top of his lungs.

Mury left the room and returned a moment later with his sensitivity plant in hand.

"You want to see sensitivity, Silva? I'll show you sensitivity." He placed the plant on the table in front of Manny and stormed out the door slamming it behind him. Without a moment's thought, Manny picked up the plant and threw it against the door.

Randy sat in stunned silence as Manny picked up what was left of the plant, threw it into the fire, and swept up the pieces of the pot and dirt and dumped them in the trash. Silently he joined Randy, who had kept a low profile during the argument, and was now turning on the television. The two men watched the screen until Mury returned about an hour later. H walked into the room and headed for the bedroom. He didn't seem to miss the plant, and made no mention of it, or the argument, was made.

Manny arrived late at the warehouse the next morning and the daily task of assembling kits had already begun. He was just pouring himself a cup of coffee when Mury came over and asked him if he had seen the sensitivity plant. Manny calmly told him what had happened.

Mury's expression was a mixture of bewilderment and pain. He looked at Manny as if he were a heartless bastard who beat up on defenseless plants. "How could you."

"You wanted to see sensitivity," Manny replied sarcastically. He expected Mury to return his smile and forget the whole incident. Instead, Mury broke into tears. His sobs far exceeded Manny's from the previous evening. All at once Mury covered his face with his arm and ran out the door with a trail of co-workers and friends after him. Manny stubbornly remained behind.

Eventually his guilt overcame him and he too, ventured out to the sidewalk. Mury, surrounded by friends trying to comfort him, looked miserable. Realizing at last, that perhaps Mury's sensitivity matched his own, Manny apologized. Shaking hands and embracing, the two men walked with the Sourdough family back into the warehouse.

Manny passed the rest of the day packing breadmaking kits and thinking of Iris. He planned to go to Union Street early and live it up with a good dinner in a fine restaurant.

Randy, once again appointed his driver, dropped Manny in front of Slater Hawkins on Union Street at eight o'clock. He dressed in brown slacks and a white turtle neck. To complete his outfit he wore leather boots and his brown cord jacket with the fur collar. As soon as Randy sped off, Manny adopted his Charles T. Short. Catching a glimpse of himself in a store window, Manny felt he looked just like the Winchester Man in the television commercial.

Manny strolled up and down the street checking out the boutiques and little shops, and now and then watching the women. The only woman who caught his eye was a small dark lady who looked to be about forty-five or fifty. She was wearing a beautiful Mexican poncho, and like Manny, she seemed to be out for a stroll. Finally, he selected a restaurant and swaggered inside.

Feeling as if everyone in the place was whispering about the mysterious handsome stranger who had just come in, Manny kept his eyes straight ahead and followed the pretty waitress to a table.

"What can I get you to drink?"

"Grandad on the rocks," Manny replied in his husky "howdy ma'am" *voice*.

The waitress quickly returned with a drink saying that she didn't know what it was, but that it sure looked powerful. Manny merely smiled and ordered a steak, very rare.

As Manny sipped his drink and waiting for his steak, he felt as if he owned the place. Casually, he looked around and checked out the women. His eyes finally met with the woman to his left who was having dinner with a Latin looking man. Ignoring her companion, the blue-eyed Portagee' smiled at the pretty lady. Her companion shot him a dirty look, but the woman responded by asking him where he came from.

"Boston," he replied.

"Really," she said. "I thought I recognized your accent. I come from Salem. You know . . . with the witches?"

Manny was asked to join them for a bottle of wine and the next hour was spent talking about Boston, and why Manny had come to San Francisco. All at once Manny noticed the time, let out a "Carrumba," and asked to be excused saying he had another engagement. Waving over the waitress he paid the bill, leaving a large tip, and bid one and all farewell. All he needed to make his exit perfect was a large cigar.

Unfortunately, when he reached Perry's, he couldn't swagger. It was too crowded. People were spilling out the door and onto the sidewalk. Squeezing through a mob of people, at least fifteen feet deep he finally saw the top of the bartender's hear. After quite a bit of maneuvering, he f.nally caught the bartender's attention by waving a twenty dollar bill. Clutching his Grandad on the tocks, Manny set out in search of Iris. No luck. She wasn't there. But then of course, it was early.

By eleven o'clock the lovesick writer had ordered another drink to quell his anxiety. The crowd had thinned out and he managed to find an empty stool. The man on his left rose to leave and was replaced a by a woman. On closer inspection, Manny saw it was the woman with the Mexican poncho he had seen earlier on Union Street. In closer proximity he could tell that she was definitely fifty. She had a thin face, not unattractive, and short curly hair beginning to grey.

"Hello," Manny said looking to pass some time.

"Hello yourself." Her voice was friendly and pleasant.

"Pretty crowded in here." Manny began the conversation with the obvious.

"It certainly is."

"You should have seen it in here earlier," Manny continued, "It was really packed. You couldn't even get near the bar."

"Perry's is the place to go for business types."

Pulling off her poncho the woman asked, "What are you doing here and what type of accent is that you have?"

Soon Manny was telling her about his book and the trip from Boston and about Sourdough Sam and Mury Nestor.

"What's your book about?"

"Cataclysms."

At the mention of cataclysms, the woman introduced herself as Sabira and the two went from strangers merely trying to pass the time, to long lost brother and sister sharing common interests.

They both talked rapidly, jumping from Edgar Cayce and Ruth Montgomery, to psychic experiences and their mutual belief in the Oneness of the Universe.

Sabira asked if Manny had heard of Wally Olly or the Sufis.

Sabira hurried on to tell Manny that he really should visit the Sufis because she felt sure he would fit right in. She worked as a secretary for them, and her experience with them had given her life new meaning. Manny explained that he had an aversion to any organized religion, but that if he had a chance, he would certainly pay them a visit.

"Well, Manny, it's time for me to go." Sabira lifter herself off the barstool and took Manny's hand in her own. Leaning close to him, she whispered, "If you ever have any trouble, get in touch with the Sufis. They'll help you."

Manny barely heard her as his mind had already returned to thoughts of Iris. "I can't see where I'm going to have any trouble, but I'll keep in mind what you said. You, take care of yourself, now."

"I will. Bye."

Perry's was nearly empty by now and a worried Manny asked the man on his right what time it was. Learning that it was midnight, Manny decided it was time to place a call to Iris. Finding no one at home, he quickly placed a call to her girlfriend, Gail.

"Hello Gail? This is Manny. Remember me? I met you and Iris at Slater Hawkins?"

"Oh, hi Manny," Gail's pleasant voice floated from the receiver. "How are you?"

"I'm fine, but have you seen Iris? She was supposed to meet me at Perry's tonight at eleven, but so far she hasn't shown up. I've tried calling her but there's no answer."

"I wouldn't hold my breath waiting for her to come."

"What do you mean?"

"I talked to Iris today and she told me she wasn't going to meet you. I told you she was a tough one to handle. She goes through men left and right. You should probably forget about her. She's on a weird trip."

Manny was crushed. The floor seemed to drop from under his feet leaving his heart and stomach in his mouth. Gail's voice brought him back to reality.

"Do you have a place to stay tonight?" She sounded concerned.

"I'd planned on spending the night with Iris. I hadn't thought beyond that."

"You're welcome to stay at my place. You could sleep on the couch."

He was still in a state of shock, but somehow he managed to take down her address and hail a cab. The driver soon deposited his shattered Winchester Man body in front of Gail's home. He felt as if he had received another mental slap in some weird mental slapstick comedy.

ELEVEN

The next morning, Gail or Bartley, as Manny had heard Iris call her, tiptoed over to the couch to hell him she was leaving for work. "Would you like a cup of tea?" Gail asked.

As if he was still in Vietnam, Manny was instantly awake and alert. "No, I think I'll take my time getting up. I'll see you later though when I bring my bags over." The previous evening Gail had offered Manny the use of her apartment for the long Thanksgiving weekend.

With a knowing and sympathetic smile, she told Manny not to worry and that everything would work out. As he heard her padding into the bathroom, Manny drifted back to sleep.

A noise in the other room brought Manny out of his sleep. Thinking he had only dozed off for a few minutes, he decided to take Gail up on her offer for tea. In the kitchen he found another roommate, the woman he had seen on the first visit to the apartment. A slim, plain looking oriental girl, who introduced herself as Sue Ling and shook his hand. The two had tea together and Manny told her Gail had offered him the use of her room for a few days. She seemed to have no objections and waved a happy goodbye as Manny left to find his way back to Sourdough Sam's.

Ned was the first person Manny encountered as he walked into Sam's. The place was a flurry of activity as the Christmas season was approaching fast. One hundred thousand kits had to be assembled and delivered to P&H who had put Sourdough Sam's on the map. Their order had to be filled.

After fortifying himself with a cup of coffee, Manny went straight to the production table to help Edna assemble the kits for packaging. Much had to be done that day as both the factory and deli would be closed the entire Thanksgiving weekend. This would be everyone's last break before the big push to get the Christmas order out on time. The closing time ping pong ritual was cancelled and a quick beer and joint substituted so everyone could get home to prepare for Thanksgiving. Everyone, except Manny, was going out of town.

Packing their respective suitcases, Manny and Mury discussed finances. "How much money have you got on you?" Mury asked while throwing his shaving kit into his suitcase.

"Ten dollars," Manny answered.

Mury tried to give Manny some more cash, but Manny refused saying he didn't feel he really needed more money as he'd be staying at Gail's. Besides, he said, he didn't want to take any more money than necessary from the family.

"Well, if you're sure. And hey, looks as if you might be able to use Ned's old apartment to write in. It is over on Second Avenue. That is if it's alright with the landlady and you like it. You could move in sometime next week. The rent is only eighty dollars a month and that includes heat and utilities. Of course, Sourdough Sam's will pick up the tab."

While Manny was pleased at the prospect of having his own place to write in, he wondered what kind of a place it might be for only eighty dollars.

As the two finished packing, Randy arrived and Mury asked him to drop Manny off at Gail's place. The two men said goodbye as Manny followed Randy out to the car. He then heard Mury call over the railing, "Don't let any purple alligators piss in your shoes."

Depositing Manny's suitcases on the sidewalk in front of Gail's house, Randy sped off calling out the window for Manny to stay out of trouble. Manny waved goodbye and headed for the doorbell. He rang once and there was no reply. He rang twice, next time pushing on the bell a little longer. Still no one came to the door. Figuring Gail must have run out to the store, Manny sat on one of his suitcases to wait for her return. After a half hour passed and there was still no sign of Gail, Manny began to get nervous.

Walking around to the side of the house, he saw a light in the window and heard a stereo blasting. Maybe she can't hear the bell over the stereo, Manny thought to himself. Just then he observed a figure pass in front of the window. What the hell is going on he wondered. He called out to Gail as loud as he could without offending the neighbors, but there was no reply. Just then he saw a second figure rush past the window. He decided it was time to take stronger action and picked up some gravel. He hurled it at the window.

Suddenly the window flew open and Gail stuck her head out. "Manny! I forgot all about you!" She was close to hysteria. "Sasha changed all the locks on the doors. When I came home and couldn't get in, I had to get a kid off the street to climb in the window."

"What are you going to do now Gail?" Manny called from the sidewalk.

"I don't know, but right now I'm packing to get out of here. She also stole some of my jewelry. I went to the landlord, but he's on her side."

"Let me in and I'll help you pack."

"Thanks, I need all the help I can get. Come around to the front and I'll unlock the door."

Once inside the house, Manny was introduced to the other figure he had see in the window. Her name was Jill and she worked with Gail. The three began packing.

"What are you going to do with your stuff after you get packed, Gail? And where are you going to go?"

"I think I can stay at my girlfriend, Joanie's for a while. I called Iris and she said the best thing was to get out before there was any more trouble. When Sasha found out you were staying here for the weekend it must have been the last straw. Although I think she had been planning to change the locks before that. I bet she was planning to keep my things in payment for the money she claims I owe her in rent."

"Are you going to take you furniture to your girlfriend's too?

"I don't know what to do about that, but I know it won't fit in Joanie's small apartment. I'm afraid to leave it here for Sasha to dump or sell."

Manny had an idea. "Listen, why don't I call over to Sourdough Sam's and see if Mury is still there. They have a big loft they aren't using, and I'm sure Mury would let you store some of your things there, at least temporarily."

"Do you really think so? Gail began to calm down.

"Of course, let's finish packing and the stuff and then you can drive it over in your car, and what doesn't fit, I'll bring over in a taxi."

"Great. Iris is on her way over to help and we can use her car too."

Manny placed the call and explained the situation to Mury. As he had hoped, Mury told him to bring the things over. When Iris arrived the group loaded most things into two cars. The only items that didn't fit were a large trunk, a box of clothes, and Manny's own suitcases.

Gail had also called another friend, Mary, and now the group of movers numbered five. When Mury answered Sourdough's bell and saw four women, headed by Manny and all carrying boxes, lamps and suitcases, his smile changed to a look of anxiety. Reassuring Mury that the women weren't moving in, but only temporarily storing the things in the loft, Manny then introduced him to Iris.

Just as he was making the introduction, Mury cut his finger on the paperclip he had been fiddling with and Iris immediately offered to play nurse. Manny was pleased that the two seemed to hit it off, but by the time the move was completed he observed a decided undertone of hostility in the interactions between the pair. He couldn't understand what had happened but assumed it had something to do with Iris's preconceived notions about Mury's homosexuality, and Mury's resentment of the way Iris had treated Manny the previous evening.

The four women decided to drive to Joanie's to plan a strategy against Sasha. And Manny, throwing his suitcases into Iris' car, went along to help. Iris was cordial in her VW and acted as if the previous evening had never happened. Although Manny was still hurt by her behavior, he still wanted to be with this woman.

Several hours later the group broke up after laying plans for a counter attack against Sasha. Gail would spend the night at Joanie's and leave for her parent's house in the morning. The third woman said she was expected some place and took her friend and left. That left Iris and Manny and the problem of what to do with him. Casually, Manny mentioned that the most logical solution would be for him to go home with Iris. Surprisingly, she agreed.

Once again Manny found himself in Iris's living room. Holding the roach clip and watching the smoke curl in the air. He wondered if the night would be an instant replay of their last evening together. The two talked for a while and finally Manny brought the subject around to sex. He told her he felt she should at least give him a try in bed, and if it didn't work, she would never have to see him again. It took nearly two more hours for the two to get undressed and into a position for lovemaking.

Lightly running his hands over her body, he could feel that her muscles were still as taut as piano wire. Deciding that was probably work tension, and not any personal animosity towards him that made her so tense and unbending, Manny resolved to win her over. Kissing her gently and massaging her shoulders, Manny began to get a response. Her body was still tight but at least there was more reaction than last time.

As he needed the muscles in her shoulders, Manny wondered what it was that attracted him to this woman. He wasn't particularly horney. Yet he wanted this woman more than any other he had ever known. He wanted to relax her, make love to her, and in turn have her fall in love with him. Unfortunately, at the rate they were going, it was going to be a tough battle. Iris was very finicky.

"Move a little closer…. Put your hand over here…. Touch my breasts…. Move your head to the left…. Ouch! Don't get my hair caught in your teeth…. You're going to fast…. I won't be able to come if you don't slow down…. Lay directly on top of me…. That's it, now faster, faster, faster oh, faster ah, that's it, that's it….uh, uh, uh, uh, I'm going to cum….No….I lost it…. Let's try again….You have to find the nugget, that's the only thing that will get me off."

Manny wasn't upset, nor did he complain. He merely took things in stride. He felt there was something special in his feelings for this woman; something that would prompt him to conquer the world for her. He started from the beginning and went through it all again. This time she made it and he had cum along with her. It wasn't the best sex he ever had, but sex wasn't all he wanted from Iris. He wanted to possess her and he wondered if this was the reaction she had on all men.

Iris moved away from him and pulled the covers around her body. Manny noticed she pulled her knees against her body as she had done that first night, almost as a small child would trying protect itself. He lay awake for nearly an hour trying to sort out his reaction to Iris. So far he had done everything he could think of to win this Libran woman. He had belittled himself in front of other men; he had put up with her standing him up, and had almost begged her to go to bed with him. Why? She gave no indication that after tonight she would ever see him again. Much less would she fall in love and move in with him. Yet, he knew he would keep trying to win her heart. What made her different than the other women he had loved?

TWELVE

Thanksgiving Day found Manny getting off the Geary Street bus and heading for Sourdough Sam's. Iris had left early that morning to spend the weekend with friends which left Manny alone with only five dollars in his pocket to get through the long holiday weekend. Maybe someone was at Sam's. His pace quickened as he noticed Rocket's Olympia Beer truck parked in front of the warehouse. Maybe Rocket hadn't gone away for the weekend and could lend the stranded writer some money, or at least let him into Mury's apartment. His hopes were quickly crushed. After he rung every bell and knocked on all the doors. Manny threw his heavy suitcases into the back of Rocket's truck and headed up the hill towards Geary Street once again

Walking without any particular direction, Manny soon found himself in the business district. Looking up he noticed a sign in a Foster's West Cafeteria; THANKSGIVING DINNER SPECIAL ONLY $2.50. Hell, thought Manny, its Thanksgiving Day, I might as well spend half of my five dollars on a turkey dinner.

The cafeteria was nearly empty except for one little old lady who was just finishing her meal. Manny deposited the contents of his tray at a table a few seats for her and began his solitary feast. He found the turkey and dressing surprisingly good, and Manny felt they were well worth half of his small fortune. He began to feel better and leaned back in his seat sipping his coffee. He then turned to the little old lady and said hello.

Returning his greeting she commented on what a nice dinner it had been and Manny countered with what a beautiful day it was for Thanksgiving. All at once he was struck with loneliness and thoughts of his family sitting around the big table at his father's house. Each year the whole clan got together and between them devoured a twenty-six pound turkey, bowls of mashed potatoes, cranberry sauce, squash and gallons of gravy. Trying to ward off his nostalgia, Manny turned to the little old lady again. "You know, I really believe Thanksgiving is a much better holiday than Christmas."

"Oh, why is that young man?"

"Well, at Christmas there is so much hassle over presents. Did I give the right thing to uncle Bob? Will he like it? Will Aunt Sue be hurt because her gift isn't as expensive? It's a pain in the neck. But at Thanksgiving you just get together with people you love and simply enjoy being together."

"You know, that's very true." The two spent the next half talking of their respective families and children. Finally the old lady said goodbye and cheerfully shuffled out the door.

As Manny went up for his third refill of coffee, he watched her walk slowly down the street until she was no longer visible. Then it hit him. Sabira and the Sufis! Didn't she say that if he ever needed help that all he had to do was go to the Sufis? Why not? What did he have to lose? He would find the Sufis!

Manny's immediate problem was how to find the Sufis. His first instinct was to return to the place where he had met Sabira. Heading in the direction of Union Street, he wondered how far it was and if he should take a bus. The bus was a quarter and he wasn't all that familiar with the transit system anyway. Instead, he retraced his steps trying to follow the route Randy had driven that night. It wasn't long before he found himself in front of the restaurant which he remembered by the wine cask out in front. Peering into the darkened building he found himself thinking of that night and his Charles T. Short swagger. His swagger was gone, the restaurant was closed, and he was no closer to finding Sabira or the Sufis.

After searching the street for a sign that would hopefully say, SUFIE HEADQUARTERS, and after having stopped several people to ask them if they had heard of such a group, Manny thought of the phone book. Unfortunately there were no Sufis listed in the yellow or white pages, but by now, Manny was on a mission and was determined to track the Sufis down.

He decided to telephone any weird sounding churches he found in the phone book, hoping they would lead him to the Sufis. The first group, CHURCH OF THE ROCK, had never heard of the Sufis, but he got lucky on his second call. The voice that answered told him to hold on a moment, and in the background he could hear people engaged in Thanksgiving festivities. Finally, another voice came on the phone and apologized for the delay.

"I'm sorry to interrupt you get-together," Manny stated.

"There's no need for apologies. What can I do for you?" The pleasant voice asked.

Manny explained about needing to find the Sufis and the man told him that Sam Lewis, who was the head of the organization, lived at number ten Pracita street. Manny thanked the man and apologized once again for the interruption. As soon as he hung-up he realized that he hadn't asked where Pracita was, or how to get there.

Walking several more blocks, Manny noticed another telephone booth in a gas station. He decided to look up Sam Lewis in the white pages. There were no listings under that name, but he happened to see a map on the wall of the service station and decided he could at least locate the correct street. Pracita seemed to be quite a distance from Union, but with the help of the station attendant he got explicit instructions on how to reach his destination via public transportation.

It was nearing five o'clock when Manny knocked on the door at number ten Pracita. Receiving no answer he decided to try the house next door. A fat balding man answered the door and told him that Sam Lewis did live next door, but that he hadn't seen him around for a long time.

Thanking the man for her information. Manny resolved to wait on Sam Lewis's doorstep, even if he had to wait all night. He'd made it this far and besides, he 'wasn't into time maannnn.' He felt like a holy man journeying through life.

Manny, alias Charles T. Short, and now a holy swami, waited and waited. He thought back to other Thanksgivings when he had been away from home and family. He'd spent one in basic training and another in Vietnam. He wondered what Susan and the kids were doing, and how Miranda was spending the day. Soon, it began to grow dark and cold. Still, he waited. He began to wonder if waiting was his vocation, and if anyone as mystically oriented as himself could possibly b waiting for nothing.

Manny guessed it had to be ten o'clock when a beat up old Rambler station wagon pulled up in front of the house. He watched as a man and woman, both dressed in flowing Indian garb and sandals got out of the car. The woman carried a baby while the short robust man with a beard and glasses went around the back of the car and began taking things out. 'Maharishi' Manny approached the man and asked if he was Sam Lewis.

"No. Sam has been dead for two years."

"Do you come from Abraham?" The bearded man asked.

"No." Manny instinctively felt that the man's question really meant, 'Are you a Sufi?'

"What do you want of me then?"

Manny quickly related his meeting with Sabira and how she had told him if he ever needed help to contact Wally Olly and the Sufis.

The man who had been watching Manny closely through his glasses, indicated for him to pick up some of the bundles and follow him. As Manny walked through the front door, the woman said sharply, "Take off your shoes."

Complying at once, Manny noticed a long row of shoes outside the door. The man quickly disappeared into the next room and the woman escorted Manny into the living room and told him to wait for Wally Olly. Then, taking the bundles from Manny, she too disappeared. Leaving Manny alone in the large room which looked more like a meeting hall than a living room as it was ringed by a circle of metal folding chairs.

Manny never saw the man enter, but all at once Wally Olly was standing in front of him asking just what the trouble was. Manny skimmed through the story emphasizing the fact he had almost no money and again Sabira's instructions to find the Sufis if he were in trouble. The man inquired how Manny had heard of Sam Lewis and after Manny explained his telephone call to the church, Wally told Manny of the circumstances of Sam's death and how he was now the head of the Sufi organization. As abruptly as he had appeared, Wally disappeared; leaving Manny to wonder what was coming next.

A few moments later, Wally returned and handed Manny part of a torn check. On the front Manny observed the man's name was printed on it and it was Walt Ali, not Wally Olli, as Manny had envisioned it in his mind. On the other side of the check was Sabira's address and telephone number. Motioning him to the phone, Walt suggested he call Sabira and see if perhaps he could stay at her house. "Hello Sabira? This is Manny

Silva. Remember me? We met on Tuesday night over at Perry's on Union Street."

"Manny? Manny…Yes, yes, the man with the deep blue eyes. Why are you calling? How did you get my number?"

Once again Manny repeated the story of his financial circumstances and homeless situation. Sabira told him that she only lived a few blocks away, and that although she had company for dinner. He was more than welcome to come over. Relieved, Manny hung up, thanked Walt Ali and started over to Sabira's.

His foot had just touched the first step when he heard another, "Take off your shoes," through the open window. The voice sounded much younger than Sabira's. As he was removing his shoes, a young woman in her twenties and dressed in hippie style clothing opened the door. Manny was introduced to the dinner company. They had their coats on and were preparing to leave. Ten minutes later Sabira and Manny were sipping coffee on the parlor floor.

Immediately, as was the case at previous meeting, Manny and Sabira slipped into an easy repose. Manny filled her in on the details of his day and also of the relationship with Iris and Mury. Sabira was particularly interested to learn that Mury was a homosexual. Pouring out the tragedy of her life she told Manny that she was deeply in love with a homosexual man who she couldn't sleep with. Manny, trying to return the kindness she had shown him, offered to fill the bill. Rather than please Sabira the suggestion upset her. She proceeded to tell Manny how at one time or another she had tried every possible sexual experiment to fill her needs; from sleeping with other women to group sex. She now felt it was her karma to wait for this one man.

After offering him the use of her sleeping bag, Sabira outlined her plans for the next day. She was going to see the Sufi Choir and the Palace of Fine Arts and offered to lend Manny the fifteen dollar admission price if he wanted to come along. The tired wanderer told her it sounded good to him and after bidding Sabira goodnight, he drifted to sleep on the living room floor wondering what the Sufi Choir could be.

***

The beautiful blonde girl on Manny's left pressed her hand into his as the Sufi Choir lifted him out of his seat with their vibrational rhythms. In the aisles, people were whirling in circles. Manny couldn't understand why they didn't fall down with dizziness. Sabira told him that was how the Sufis of India had earned their nickname, whirling dervishes.

Never in his life had Manny heard anything like the Sufi Choir. Beethoven's Ninth Symphony done in full orchestra could only hope to get people half as high as the choir before him. The choir alone was worth the fifteen dollar admission price, but the events of the weekend seemed tailor made for Manny. There would be lectures on pyramids and auras, a showing of the firs, a Kirilian film from the Soviet Union of an aura on a photographic plate, another new film called Chariot of the Gods by a man named Von Daniken, and a lecture on Atlantis by a Venezuelan scientist. Even the lobby was a show in itself: vendors lined the corridors selling everything from popcorn to aluminum pyramids. On manufacturer claimed that if a person slept under a pyramid for three months, he would become a vegetarian. Books on every religion imaginable were for sale, as well as gadgets to measure how far an aura extends for a person's body.

Manny even met a woman, the pretty blonde who had held his hand during the choir singing. She was a friend of Sabira and her name was Patricia. She and Manny got into a heavy philosophical discussion about religion. As the weekend drew to a close and he and Sabira prepared to leave. Pat took his hand and told him she was a Theosophist.

"Remember," she whispered. "If you ever need help, come and see the Theosophists."

THIRTEEN

When Manny returned to Sourdough Sam's on Monday morning, the luggage which he had left in Rocket's beer truck was waiting for him inside the door. Mury, who had worried at the sight of the luggage and no Manny, was relieved to see him. He listened with interest as Manny described the eventful weekend he had had. Manny's heart leapt for joy as Mury informed him that Iris had called and said she would try again later. Next Mury asked if Manny would like to take a ride to see Ned's apartment.

"You can check it out and see if you think it's suitable for a budding young Portagee' writer."

They drove over to Ned's in Bobby's fast and sleek sports car. At least ten speakers were set up in the car and as Manny and Mury sped along the street, 'Love Unlimited' blared forth. The tune was Mury and Bobby's love song.

As Mury had predicted, Ned's place was perfect for a writer. The furnished rooms were located in the basement of a house owned by a woman who had lived in San Francisco since the time of the big 'quake'. As she lived alone, she was pleased with the idea of having a man around. Ned spent most of his time in San Jose and she really wanted someone like Manny who would be around more often.

It was agreed that if Ned could move his things out the next day, Manny could move right in. The news pleased him as he was anxious to get started on his book. Mury asked if Manny would need anything for the apartment and Manny said that the only things he really needed were some underwear and a pair of pajamas. Mury agree to take him shopping. Mury would have taken him right then, but Manny was anxious to get back to Sam's and wait for Iris's call.

***

Dear Miranda

Well, here I am. It's my first morning in my own apartment. Excuse me a second, I want to finish making my bed….All done. You should see this place! Edgar Allan Poe would have had a hard time finding a better place to write. This friend of mine, Mury, brought me here last night. (Mury is the guy who got me out to San Francisco.) The place is really cool. (It has no heat.) But other than that I like it. To get in here you have to walk through this long passageway which goes under the house in front of this one. (Keep your head low.) It's very dark and the light switch is on the other end of the tunnel. Then you open this little door which looks like it doesn't lead anywhere and you're into my place. (My hands are cold and I'm having a little trouble with the typewriter.) At any rate as you walk into the front room you look to the right and all of a sudden you see a writer's heaven. The place is so tiny and funky there has to be magic in it.

The apartment has two rooms and a bath. It's all done in knotty pine like my living room at home, only with no finish on the wood. The kitchen is a good size room (It also has the bedroom dresser it.) The table I am writing on is opposite the door and in a corner and behind me is the sink, stove, and fridge. If you look directly opposite where I'm sitting, you can see the corner of the bedroom and the bed. There is a small night table and a big reclining chair which vibrates. I guess that's all I have to tell you about the rooms except that this being in the basement it gives the feeling that the entire floor is on a slant. (Oh God, I wish you were here.)

How have you been? Did you get my first letter? I was afraid you might throw it away as it was in a Sourdough Sam envelope. I thought you might think it was an advertisement. I'm going to leave you a few minutes to get some food. I'm starved.

Here I am again. This cup of coffee tastes sooo..good. I put a couple of eggs to boil on the stove. I love you. Why don't you move out here with me? How are things going with you and your husband, William? All set to move back to Chicago? How are the Bedford Farms Players and Jack and Peter doing?

San Francisco is a magic city. I love it. I just can't explain the feeling this city gives me. As much as I have missed everyone, I haven't been the least bit lonely. (Well, maybe just a little.) Oh, I don't have any homosexual problems at all. The first night, Mury asked me to sleep in his bed and I said I would, but only to sleep, nothing else. All night he tried to get me to perform, but I wouldn't do it. We had a long talk. (one of many) Finally he realized that it just wasn't my bag. (At least for now.) So, my book is still on and today I will start it. I would like to finish it by the middle of January if it's at all possible, and at that time I will head home until promotions for the book begin.

There are so many things I have to tell you. The trip out here was unbelievable and the trip I've been on since I got here even more unbelievable. (My eggs must be ready. I think I will eat now.)

Hello again. It must be nearly two hours since I last wrote to you. I don't have a watch or a clock here and the only way I know the date is because there's a calendar on the wall. I was sitting in my reclining chair eating my second sandwich when I realized that I may have sent my last letter to you in Lowell instead of Bedford Farms. Damn it! I bet I did. At any rate, I didn't say much in it except that I was safe and I loved you very much. (This typewriter makes a lot of noise.)

Will you do me two favors? First, although I know you don't want to get involved, could you please convince Susan to move into my house? I've asked her but she keeps stalling. I told her she could have the place until next September, but she won't give me any answer. I even told her she could have my unemployment checks for the mortgage. (My expenses here are being taken care of by Sourdough Sam's.) I would feel so much better knowing that she and the kids were living in the house. If there is anything you could do to convince her, I would really appreciate it. When I go back home I can always find another place to live. Now, second favor. Will you send me John Cook's address? Thank you.

I'm not going to tell you all the trips I have been going through, but I promise to go into it another time. Right now I think I will get to my book.

Love Manny xxxxxxxxoooooooooooo

***

Manny's second letter to Miranda left him physically and emotionally drained. The last two weeks before the trip, they had grown closer than ever. Constant companions on the movie set; they made love at every private moment. Leaning back in the recliner, Manny wondered how Miranda would react to Iris.

Miranda was aware that he saw other women back home, but she also knew she was the one he wanted most. Manny recalled their last few days together and how much he had wanted to tell her to leave her husband and kids and come away with him. He knew in his heart it was impossible and so would she. He switched on the vibrating recliner and the gentle motion soother him. God, he thought, and felt how much he missed Miranda. Right now he wanted to hold her. The tears began to flow. He had to get out of the apartment to clear his head. He decided to go for a walk.

The apartment was on Second Avenue and only a ten minute bus ride up Clement to Sourdough Sam's. As he walked around his new neighborhood, Manny fell in love with the entire area. This was a part of San Francisco that was just coming to life. Tiny vegetable stands, small cozy bars, and sidewalk cafes dotted the streets. Manny sat at one of the outdoor cafes sipping red wine in the warmth of the sun, and thought that no writer could possibly ask for a better place to ply his trade. His thoughts then turned to his book.

He had to get the book done, and it had to be a success. He had to do it for Mury, for the sourdough family, for himself, and for the world, but especially for Iris. She wanted a man of accomplishment and not some adventurer or would-be unpublished writer. The last time he had seen Mury, he advised him to just let his writing flow and worry about the spelling and grammar on the rewrite. He also had mentioned the dope deal again.

Manny had told Mury that he was going to have to call home for the phone numbers of certain people regarding the cocaine. He also had some questions for Mury like; "Should I call people at home of at work? Should I call from Sourdough's, or was that too dangerous?" Manny wasn't planning on giving out any information as to who he was working for or where he was staying. Mury had told him, "We must keep the cocaine deal compartmentalized. No one at Sam's knows about this deal except you, me, and Bobby. We want to keep it that way."

As Manny sipped the last of the wine, he thought to himself. If my contact won't know anything about Sourdough Sam's, it's best Mury doesn't know who he is. At any rate, I had better start doing some calling soon, and I had better get some writing done. Paying his tab he went back to his apartment.

Later that night, with the dope deal back in his mind, Manny caught the Clement Street bus to Sam's. Finding the downstairs door unlocked, Manny made his way upstairs to the apartment. He found Mury reading in bed.

"Hello," Manny said unemotionally, and then a split second later in a very emotional voice he said, "I know we can pull this dope deal off." Then he threw his arms around the surprised manager. The two men made a pact to solidarity, vowing to go to jail, or die before they would sell the other out. They were to be brothers to the end.

Moving into the living room the two men began their first detailed discussion on how the cocaine deal was to proceed. How much cocaine should they buy? How much would it cost? How much could they sell it for?

It was agreed that after Manny phoned his contact back East in order to lay the groundwork for the sale, he would travel home at Christmas under the guise of delivering completed breadmaking kits. While there, he could settle the final arrangements for the sale. It sounded like a good idea to Manny and it would also give him a chance to see his family and friends. Also he could bring back a few of his belongings.

Mury then raised the question of Manny' involvement with Lenny's wife, Flo. Mury wanted to know if Manny had been having an affair with her. Manny said that he had, but told Mury it had ended last summer. Mury said he had guessed as much.

Manny asked if Mury was thinking of bringing Lenny into the dope deal and wondered if that was why Mury had asked about the affair.

"I'm thinking about it." Mury replied.

"I don't think that's such a good idea." Manny countered.

"I haven't made up my mind yet."

"I don't feel that Lenny is emotionally stable. He told me that he double crossed business partners of his in the past. Also Flo told me he had been involved with the FBI in the past."

"I don't think Lenny has enough brains to cause us any problems. Besides, you let me worry about that. As business manager, that's my decision."

Mury sounded confident and positive. Manny let the subject drop and Mury filled a pipe with pot. After lighting up, Mury handed the pipe to Manny and announced that he was throwing a birthday bash for himself on December fifteenth. He added, "Everyone at Sam's is invited, Rocket too." Mury's mention of Rocket turned him back to the cocaine deal.

Manny spoke up first. "I'm going to have to call home to get the number of our first contact."

"Why don't you call right now?" Mury said that once a project began he liked to more quickly.

"Not tonight." Manny added quickly. "It's too late back there with the time difference. I'll call in the morning."

Without saying more on the subject, Mury inquired about Iris. "How are things going with your old lady?"

"I'd hardly call her my old lady yet," Manny replied. "But we are getting along much better. She's picking me up here tomorrow night to show me the sights of San Francisco. If you can lay a few bucks on me. I'd like to take her to the Cliff House for a few drinks and to watch the sunset and then to Victoria Station for dinner."

"Ah, you're falling in love, you silly Portagee'." Mury flashed a toothy smile at the Pisces.

"What do you mean falling," Manny laughed, "I fell." Manny paused for a moment and added, "I'm going to tell her about the cocaine deal."

"Do you think that's a good idea?" Mury's tone was serious.

"Why not? I think she can be trusted. Besides, when things start getting heavy, it'd be nice to have a little moral support. I know she can handle it." Manny felt strongly that Iris was born for adventure.

"Do what you feel is right, but don't let things get out of hand with her. She just might freak out."

"I doubt it. You're forgetting this is the woman who traveled through Vietnam and hitch hiked through the Mid East during the war. She's a pretty together lady. She'll love the excitement."

Mury did not sound impressed or reassured. "She seemed okay in the brief time I talked to her. What do you think made her change her mind about seeing you?"

"I'm not sure," Manny replied. "I think it had something to do with her sign. Librans are hard to peg. When I pushed too see her, she ignored me.

But when I ignored her, she started to be interested. Susan and Miranda are Librans too. They're the same way. It's a hell of a sign to deal with. If you have a problem with these women, like a fight or something, they simply float off to their ivory towers. You can't touch them until they decide to come down."

Mury just shook his head.

FOURTEEN

The two lovers sipped their Irish coffees as the sun dipped into the Pacific and watched the seals below scrambling out of the water onto the rocks. Earlier, Iris had picked Manny up at Sam's for their first "real" date, and told him she planned to take him to visit some funky little places away from the tourist traps. She consented to bring him to the Cliff House because she felt that although it was a tourist highlight, it was well worth a visit.

Perched on the side of a cliff at the entrance to San Francisco Bay, the Cliff House boasted one of the finest reputations for elegant dining since 1858. The lounge where Manny and Iris were sipping drinks was furnished with small tables and a variety of love seats and high-backed wicker chairs. The high wooden-framed windows afforded a panoramic view of the Pacific Ocean. The effect out the window as the sun dipped its last rays into the water was spectacular.

The Ivory Tower, as Manny had christened Iris in his mind, and the Pisces sat near the window talking of old lovers. Although there wasn't the intimacy of lovers in their relationship yet, they did have an easy feeling between them and there was no awkwardness in their conversation. He spoke to her of his writing and his aspirations for success. She told him of her law suit and the difficult time men had given her in the business world. Being a single woman, she had worked hard all her life and now she longed to be taken care of with no day to day worries about how to make a car payment or pay the rent. She wanted to find some man to take care of those things and leave her free to travel the world. She longed to be carefree, relaxing in the sun on some deserted beach in Mexico, or spending her days tripping through little shops of Europe.

"You might be able to do that someday," Manny answered trying to offer her hope and reassurance. He felt as he listened to her dreams that he understood more of her tensions.

"How? Do you know a millionaire who will support me but leave me alone at the same time? I couldn't stand to make love to some shriveled up old man, my men have to be perfect lovers or I throw them right out."

"Well, when the cocaine deal goes through, you won't have to look for any shriveled up old millionaires." Manny flashed her a wide smile. He wanted her to be happy, and he wanted to be the one to make her so, no matter what the price.

"I'll believe that when I see the money. That friend of yours, Rocket, is a crazy character. I don't know if I would trust him as far as I could throw him." Something in her judgmental tone made Manny defensive.

"I know he seems crazy, but both Mury and I feel he just needs one break to make good. You can't deny that there aren't some very 'real' things about him. You saw him balance that table on his chin."

Iris looked skeptical, and as Manny didn't want to hear any negative comments about the deal, or Rocket, he ignored her comments. He knew he would need all the positive energy possible to pull this deal off.

Changing the subject, he said, "Speaking of tables Luv, if we don't get to Victoria Station soon, there won't be any left."

Victoria Station was just as Manny had remembered from his dinner there with Mury. Crowds of people, deep red carpets, and lot soft dark wood combined to make a perfect atmosphere. With delicious dinner and several more drinks in them, Manny and Iris began to feel more like lovers. As they finished the last of their coffee, Iris suggested they head back to her place for brandy and a doobie.

Passing the joint to Manny, Iris left to find a bottle of Courvoisier. Manny's thoughts strayed back to Pinckney Street on Beacon Hill in Boston. He remembered a bottle of cognac he had shared with a lover on their first date. One sniff of the heady aroma had taken his breath away. Now, sniffing the Courvoisier, he noticed the aroma wasn't as sharp, but as he took his first sip, he would feel the heat spreading through his body all the way to his genitals.

The first kiss, only a peck, happened in the living room floor in the middle of a conversation. More conversation and then, at the end of a sentence, another kiss, this one lingering longer than the first. Iris suggested another doobie and a "tad" more brandy. Iris always used the expression, tad, for a small amount, and the expression amused Manny. He teased her about still having elements of a farm girl about her. Passing the doobie back and forth, they shared more kisses.

Manny began to feel the strange sensation he had before some lovemaking. The feeling only hit him on certain occasions and with certain women. It always started slowly and registered first about three or four feet behind his head. He could never attach a name to the feeling as it was more a presence that he sensed. Perhaps, waves came closest to describing the pleasant sensations. At any rate, the waves were coming now and moving from the left side of his head and all the way around the other side, surrounding him and moving downward until they filled his entire body. As the feeling reached this groin, the waves began moving upward again, gathering speed and intensity until they burst through his eyes and into the first and nearest willing receptacle. In this case, the receptacle was Iris' eyes. The waves entered her, consuming her entire body and flowed back to Manny though her mouth. Soon the two were kissing, long moist kisses, filled with feelings so powerful they electrified their tongues.

Pulling back, Iris said, "Why don't you roll another doobie while I get a glass of water to take into the bedroom with us."

"Fer sure." Manny answered reaching for the plastic bag on the black streamer trunk. By the time Manny had finished rolling the joint and had joined Iris in the bedroom, she was already between the sheets. She drank some of the water, and as she replaced the glass on the night stand, she told Manny that he would have to get the next glass. Thinking she was joking and wondering what has happened to the mood from the living room, Manny laughed. Iris told him she wasn't kidding and that if he wanted more water he would have to get it. Disappointed that the magic spell between them had been broken, Manny tried to lighten the conversation.

"Okay. I realize as a Libran, you need to have things balance."

"Cut the astrology shit, and get your ass in bed, Silva."

"Yes sir, I mean ma'am," Manny replied and quickly jumped into the bed beside her.

Iris had placed the ashtray between them on the bed, and as they passed the joint back and forth they inhaled deeply, drawing the pungent smoke deep into their lungs. As they exhaled, they opened their mouths wide, causing the smoke to push up and out. Each new exhalation caused a wave of sexuality to grow between them. Soon, each drag of the joint was interrupted by tongue touching tongue and lips meeting lips. All at once, the ashtray was gone, the lights were out, and the room seemed to have vanished. The only reality was their lips touching as the two became one.

The lips found their way down necks and across shoulders, licking and sucking and taking little bites as they went. They felt arms and fingers and back up to the shoulders and down to breasts. Nipples were erect, firm and supple. One pair of lips was invited lower. They slid over a tummy, lingering at the small opening in the stomach. Around the side they traveled to the fleshy parts, kissing a hip biting a cheek. Little gasps and "ahaas" and little grasps of "oos" escaped as the lips flowed around the hips to the soft inner thighs.

Between the thighs more lips joined in. They lifted, parted and came alive with their own sweet saliva. A tongue licked the new lips and found its way into the throat and then back out. More kissing and sucking and the lips moved again. Up through soft pubic hair, up to the heaving tummy with the small hole, up to where they could suck nipples again and back to their mates.

As mouths touched again the lips between the thighs opened beckoning in a cock. It didn't need help; it didn't need guidance. It found its own way to the lower lips that sucked it in like a popsicle on a hot summer's day. More lips parted and words came out. "Leave it here and don't move for a while." It didn't.

Now the lips were gone and there was only a single body. At first it didn't move, and then slowly, very slowly, it took on a pulse. It moved ever so slightly. That move brought on another move and in turn another. The move became a beat, the beat became a stroke. The body was alive. It was moving, up and down, in and out, mounting pressure, don't stop now, can't stop now. Steady movement steady movement steady movement . . moov . . . ommooo . . . . oooo . . . . ooooooh . . . . ohhh . . . ooh . . . oh . . . oooooooooohhhhh . . . .

Manny couldn't hold it any longer. The cum came in big whooshes from somewhere deep inside. With each stroke a bigger whoosh, and with each whoosh, a deeper stroke. His hips went down and his cock went up. Up up up until he felt her completely filled. One more whoosh and collapse. . . .

They lay still for a long time. When they could finally move, they looked at each other. Manny said, "Hello. Who are you?"

"My name is Michelle."

"Michelle. That's such a soft feminine name."

"That's what I am."

Gone now was Iris, Gone now was the caustic tongue and the piano wire muscles. In her place was Michelle and Manny spent the rest of the weekend with her.

They didn't do work. They didn't argue. They didn't go out. All they did was eat big sumptuous breakfasts of bacon and eggs with homemade rolls and jam; lunches of egg salad with mayonnaise, mustard, onion and pickles, and heavy dinners of lamb shanks stuffer with garlic and onion. He ate her spicy food and loved it. All of this they did staying in bed except to do the cooking or change the record on the stereo. But mostly they made love.

Fast love, slow love, love to music; love with her on top, then him. Love upside down, right side up, moving, turning, him saying, "I love you Michelle," as they fell asleep in each other's arms Sunday night.

FIFTEEN

"Hello, Liquidated Fiduciaries Unlimited. May I help you?"

"Yes, I'd like to speak to Al Silva, please. I'm calling long distance."

"Who may I say is calling?"

"Manny Silva."

"Hold on a minute, please."

Manny knew Al from the family, they were cousins and had practically grown up together. Although Al was a few years older, Manny saw quite a lot of him as he hung around with Al's younger brother, Steve. Their two families were still in touch and Manny knew through the grapevine where Al was working. Manny wasn't absolutely positive that Al could help with the cocaine connection, but he did know that Al had been involved in some pretty shady deals. He's done time for possession of large quantities of marijuana and at one time had shared a jail cell with Jimmy Hoffa. Manny felt if anyone could handle this type of deal, it was Al. The man owned a string of race horses and never drove anything less expensive than a Jaguar. Manny felt he didn't get that kind of money from his job at Liquidated Fiduciaries. Suddenly, the phone came alive.

"Manny, how the hell are you?"

"Pretty good, Al. Pretty good."

"I hear you've been out to the West Coast. Where are you calling from?"

"I'm calling from a pay phone in San Francisco."

"That's a long way from home. What can I do for you?"

What could Al do for him? Manny wondered. The last time he had seen Al, the man had offered him a large commission if he could find a buyer for some land on Cape Cod. Manny wasn't able to oblige, but he later read in the paper that a piece of real estate similar to the one Al had been trying to unload had come under suspicion in relation to the buyers and sellers. A group on the Cape had formed to block the sale and the Kennedy family was part of that group.

"Al, I don't know exactly how to put this . . . on your phone?"

"Yah, it's safe. What have you got?"

"I'm involved in a one shot deal to unload a large quantity of snow. Do you know anyone who might want to make a buy?"

Al was silent a few moments. "I might. How much are we talking about?"

"I'm not sure yet, but it would be pounds . . . ."

"Sounds like a heavy deal. It might call for some real bucks. I couldn't handle it by myself."

"But do you know people who could?"

"Yah. Listen, why don't you get back to me again. In the meantime I'll scout around and see what I can come up with."

"I'll do better that that. I'm coming home for Christmas and I'll drop by and see you."

"Great."

"Okay, then. You'll hear from me again when I get in town."

"Take care of yourself, Manny. Thanks for calling."

Manny hung up and dialed Mury's number. He informed his manager that the ball was rolling. With the phone call off his mind, he headed back to his room to begin writing.

The book Manny was writing was about his family's turmoil as they tried to reach southern Illinois after the cataclysms had been going for quite a while. Ned's apartment had turned out to be a small dry cell battery for the fledgling writer. The energy flowed through him as he wrote, pouring out onto the paper. He was up to chapter six and about to describe the day he and his brother were smoking pot when he ran into writer's block. Somehow he could not capture the feeling of being stoned using words. He quickly rolled up a small joint, smoked it, and headed back to the typewriter full of confidence and inspiration.

He placed his fingers on the electric typewriter and instead of the intended scene; strange words began to jump out.

"in the early days before man was in the form he is now, he was an amoeba-like creature elected to live on land, while others decided to remind in the sea. Those who remained in the sea evolved into fish, while those who remained on land evolved into Man. Forget trying to talk to dolphins by mechanical means, speak to them with mental telepathy."

Manny didn't know what this writing meant, or where it had come from. He put his hands back on the keys and tried again.

". . . . grabbed some people at the same time and saw them as cells with lives surrounding them like ectoplasm . . . contained Mury, Iris, and Manny. Each was their nucleus with the rest of the cell being their relationships, or what they had been through in this life. Outer part of cell was the feeling of outer level of consciousness where you give off or feel and either take in energy or release it . . . High energy levels are . . . sensitivity. The meek shall inherit the earth . . . Things won't change much in the coming years due to a depression. Things will stagnate . . . short period of Dark Ages. You predicted for two years a return to conservatism. . can hold you back as well as change fashion and politics."

Suddenly the writing stopped. Reading over what he wrote, Manny tore the paper from the IBM and rushed to the bus stop heading for Sourdough Sam's. He had to show this to Mury.

Mury was astounded when he read the statements Manny had written about him. He felt sure that the writing was some kind of sign that meant that the cocaine deal was a righteous trip. The two men heard voices downstairs that indicated it was closing time in the factory. Manny, in a pious mood thought about his writing feat. He donned a table cloth over his head and rushed downstairs to bless the forthcoming ping pong match with a few sprinkles of Compari and tonic.

Excited by yesterday's writing session, Manny headed for his typewriter the first thing the next morning. This time, with no prodding from pot, more automatic writing poured from the keys.

"In the early days before man was in the form he is in now, he was an amoeba-like creature which split to reproduce . . . When we discover what the sub-atom looks like; we will find it looks the same as the atom. Beneath that, it keeps going and going, same as space and universe structure in the other direction . . . Sickness is the stoppage of the natural flow of energy . . . A pyramid builds to a point with the base connected to earth. It is doing the same thing in retrospect, making a connection between, sub-atom to universal, like fuse to fuse box . . . Atlantean crystal did the same thing, tapping a huge conscious energy and projecting it deep into sub-atom, multiplying levels of consciousness and energy. The more levels of consciousness you can reach, the more energy forces you are able to tap . . . the aura of earth shows a burst of positive forces are needed to continue the flow . . . Earth movements are part of the atom-earth health movement. As man tries to clean himself, so does earth. Happening on all levels . . . YOU SEE. . You see. . . Cleansing of sub-atom is bringing about rebirth of religious and psychic beliefs . . . ONE IN SAME. . ."

Manny paused for a moment to catch his breath and then resumed his position at the typewriter.

> ". . .The more sensitive you let yourself become, the larger the energy field . . . because sensitivity is strength . . . Large nuclear power can't do anything against small agricultural country; same as muscle-bound to pencil . . . If you are in a battle you put up a defense, a defense is a barrier . . . won't let anything come in , or go out . . . You cease to flow because flow goes in all directions in and out . . . Three dimensional life gives you a body which is a shell or the outside of an atom, The outer skin of defense . . . MUST BREAK OUT OF THE BODY TO OPEN UP BODY TO SENSITIVITY. SHOWER POWER. . . Cleansing isn't just cleaning, it is also rejuvenation. . . for every action, etc. . . . . As shower is cleansing you it is also taking off excess energy . . . Taking is giving and giving

taking . . . Works same as cataclysms will on earth . . . The earth will be rejuvenated, releasing new energy and new life.

If you and Iris were to take a shower together at the beginning of EACH MEETING . . . you would neutralize your negative excess energy and flow into ONE … Humans must learn to be one with their own kind before they can be one with everything . . . Don't be afraid to talk with mate and people . . . If they can't understand you, you can't understand them . . . Lack of communication is the biggest cause of confusion . . . To communicate telepathically, you have to rid yourself of all fears that you will misunderstand what the other person is saying.

Know you are right . . . know everything you are thinking and doing is right . . . You can do this by being honest with yourself . . . Become ONE with yourself . . . You are a single atom even if you are part of a whole which is also an atom in itself . . . Knowing yourself and being truthful with yourself is necessary to know when you should die . . . Until humans can be truthful with themselves, they won't have any control over when they die . . . Thus, no control over their own evolution.

The entire revolutionary process in man is one atom or one life. If you stop your life, you stop your own evolution and the evolution of the world, and vice versa."

As mysteriously as the writing had begun, it ended. Manny, completely exhausted, laid his head down on the table.

SIXTEEN

Manny spent the morning of December fifteenth riding over to Sourdough Sam's to procure an ounce of grass. A pound of pot was always kept on hand for family use, and Manny needed it to put into the brownies he planned to bake for Mury's birthday bash that night.

It took him the better part of that afternoon to make his specialty, but between sifting the grass, mixing it into the batter and trying to find the proper oven temperature, Manny even managed to write a letter to Susan and the kids.

Because his children were still too young to read, Manny sent letters to them in picture form. Occasionally, he would receive a picture in return, sandwiched between the pages from Susan. Those he carefully tucked away. The stick figures with pie-shaped clown faces never failed to bring tears to his eyes. As he ended his letter to them with hugs and kisses, he felt the lump rising in his throat and quickly climber into the shower to push away the feelings.

Manny arrived at Sam's early enough to help with last minute preparations. Along with his brownies, he carried a special present for Mury from Sabira. She and Manny had been seeing quite a lot of each other since their weekend at the Palace of Fine Arts. She even had been taking Manny to healing classes at the Sufi Center. At one of these sessions while Manny was trying to direct the group's healing energy back to Massachusetts where his son, Google, was having breathing difficulties, a bolt of lightning-like electricity had surged around the room. Later his wife Susan had written that the sessions may have helped because shortly afterwards, Goggle's breathing problem cleared up. However, it wasn't psychic energy that Sabira had sent to Mury, it was a tab of acid that her homosexual boyfriend had given her. Sabira felt it was just the gift for Mury. Neither Mury nor Manny had every done acid, and Manny felt tonight might be a good time to take their first trip. He had recently finished reading Tom Wolf's 'Electric Kool-Aid Acid Test', and was looking forward to the experience.

Expecting to be the first guest to arrive, Manny burst through the door with a hearty, "Happy Birthday, Mury," only to find Mury doing his first line of cocaine with his brother and sister-in-law. Manny was offered a line, introduced, and the party began.

After Manny had finished his first drink, the group went downstairs to set out the food. Mury had laid in a supply of cocaine, champagne and liquor. The two enormous speakers from the bedroom had been set up in the general store area for dancing. Mury expected the party to spread into the warehouse and throughout the building as it grew. Manny stared at the impressive array of dope arranged on the long countertop. Never before, not even in Vietnam, had he seen such a display. Mury had decided to share his acid with anyone who wanted to try it, so a bowl of punch was quickly mixed, and a sign stating; 'CAUTION, DRINK AT YOUR OWN RISK,' was attached. Earlier, Bobby, Jerry and Margo had pushed tables and shelves against the wall and hung streamers from every conceivable place. Manny even noticed another batch of brownies.

Soon Iris arrived, almost acting her Michelle personality, and after her, Randy, with his girlfriend, Jennie. Next, Rocket true to his name shot through the door accompanied by his pretty 'old lady'. He immediately went into his balancing act which ended with a flourish as he picked up Randy's girlfriend, Jennie, and balance her on his chin.

The carpenter with the Jesus-like beard arrived and with him a roofer named Phil. Gail, Iris' girlfriend, appeared and froze the group with a scream as she recognized Phil as an old friend she had known in Africa. Apparently before he became a roofer, he had been a diplomat. More people arrived and soon the party grew too large for introductions. Manny sampled a few brownies, washed those down with a few glasses of punch, and added several glasses of champagne for a chaser. Jennie was attracting everyone's attention in her low cut blue sheath and Bobby and Mury were doing their love dance while laughter mixed with the sounds of "Love Unlimited" blaring through the speakers to the accompaniment of the clatter of ping pong. Kohoutek was really doing a job of pulling extreme type of people together.

Manny had no idea what time it was when Iris suggested they take a walk. Grabbing the first bottle of champagne he found, the two headed for San Francisco Bay. They had only walked three blocks in the cold wind when they decided against going any further and the bottle of champagne concurred by popping its cork, unaided. Instead, they decided to take Iris' car over to Manny's apartment. Iris insisted she was too drunk to drive, so Manny jumped behind the wheel and started the ignition.

Manny didn't feel the least bit high and was undisturbed as the cars and buildings seemed to jump in front of the VW and then quickly scurry back where they came from. Manny found a parking place directly in front of his apartment, something nearly unheard of in San Francisco. Putting the car in reverse, he turned to see where he was going but was unable to move as torrents of laughter suddenly burst from his mouth. He couldn't imagine why the process of parking suddenly seemed so funny. Calming himself, he shifted and tried again, only to be engulfed by more laughter. After his fifth try, Iris, who didn't see the humor of the situation, got out and insisted Manny let her park the car. He complied, composing himself in the process. He couldn't let Iris know he was having any reaction to the acid. Besides, he didn't think he was. Manny was used to handling himself in all situations. After all, hadn't he behaved coolly when he discussed the cocaine deal with Rocket? He'd played the role of the young Mafia Don with perfect aplomb and coolly told Murray that he could 'step on' the fifteen pound of cocaine which would double its weight and thus, its price. Certainly, he could control a simple acid trip.

As Iris parked the car, thoughts of the cocaine deal flooded Manny's mind and he began to grow paranoid. On one hand the deal sounded simple and straightforward. On the other hand, although he knew Al, he was not sure who Al's contact was. Could it possibly be the Mafia? Could he even be killed? His thoughts were interrupted as Iris slammed the car door.

As soon as they were inside the apartment, Iris told Manny she wouldn't be able to spend the night with him, as her mother had arrived from North Dakota and would be expecting her home. Manny, once again in a good mood, kidded her about the fact that a thirty-three year old woman still had to worry about what her mother might think. Iris' response was short and to the point.

"Cut the shit, and get into bed."

Happy to comply with her request, Manny slid between the sheets and turned to kiss her. Suddenly, the scene of Iris's mother waiting at home for her brought more gales of laughter. He laughed so hard, tears streamed down his face. The scene of Iris's mother soon gave way to other scenes. It seemed as if every far out thought he had ever had was zooming through his mind at lightning speed. His head was moving a mile a minute and each thought produced a scene of incredible color. Emotions replace thoughts, and laughter was replaced by crying.

Remembering Iris, and fearing he might be freaking her out, he forced himself to calm down. However by this time Iris was good and mad, and Manny couldn't seem to understand why. Then it struck him. Iris was kissing him. Did she want to make love? Could that be what she wanted? His mind stopped running in circles and began to focus on one idea. Perhaps this acid was controllable after all, just like grass. Could he make it do what he wanted? Could he control it?

Manny didn't ask any more questions. He saw a button on his chest marked SEX and pushed it. As he turned to Iris, her mouth swallowed his tongue, and the sensation was incredible. He felt as if they were two amoebas swimming in a drop of water and breaking into each other's protoplasm. They seemed to be one blob of sex.

The feelings were overwhelming now. He was on her. She was on him. They were moving, building, mounting. Setting on top of him she began writhing. He could see her face, her breasts, and her body. He could ever see into her stomach, into her appendix, her intestines, and into her vagina where his cock was sliding, pulsating, pumping in and out.

Gasps came from Iris's mouth, groans from Manny's. The earth wasn't just moving under them, it was quaking and shaking. Manny could see his erection expanding and filling the whole lower half of her body. The grasps and groans had grown to screams. Manny felt the muscles behind his testicles began to tighten then release. His muscles began pumping and something was being pushed out. His cock expanded again filling the entire inside of her body when it finally exploded! Sparks like a fourth of

July fireworks display burst out of the top of her transparent head!! Then again and again and again. . . until the two crumpled in exhaustion.

The spent couple lay quietly for only a short time before Manny's head began tripping again. Once again, he began the laughing and crying. In order not to frighten Iris and to calm himself down, he saw the magic sex button and pushed it again.

When he had pushed it for the last time, it was after six-thirty in the morning, and Iris had to leave. Manny tried to convince her to stay, but she was adamant.

As the door shut, Manny felt the waves in his brain change gears. He tried to sleep, but couldn't. He wasn't the least bit tired, although he knew he should be. Instead, he felt as if his body was speeding. He couldn't make up his mind what to do.

Should I get up . . . No. What could I do . . . take a shower? Get dressed . . . I have to do something. Doughnuts. I want doughnuts. I'll go see Mury; maybe he wants some doughnuts, too.

Manny arrived at the bus stop at the exact moment the bus pulled up. It seemed as if he had just sat down when it was time to get off at his stop. At Mury's the door was unlocked, and Manny walked in. There was no noise in the apartment, but the bedroom door was wide open. "Doughnuts, do you want some doughnuts?" Manny yelled as he burst through the door and jumped on the bed.

Bobby and Mury had been trying to sleep, and they complained at the intrusion.

"Do you want some doughnuts?" Manny was firm.

Getting out of bed they complained, dressing they complained, and on the way out to the car they were still complaining, but as they dropped Manny off at the doughnut shop, they were laughing as they drove away.

Inside the shop, the doughnuts jumped off the counter at Manny, while the smell of freshly baked pastry nearly knocked him off his feet. He felt in his pocket for money and pulled out a bill sending change flying in all directions. He felt as if every person in the shop must know he was tripping. He drank his coffee, ate four doughnuts, and left.

What now, he thought. Where can I go? He immediately thought of Iris, but wondered how he could get to her house.

Walk. And so he did. He knew that Mission Street lead to Daly City so he headed in that direction. Passing a small second hand shop, he was struck by something in the window. Pressing his nose to the window, he saw it was a plastic statue of a naked cupid boy, but in place of the usual fig leaf covering the genitals was a small hole where a tiny light bulb could be screwed in. Deciding to bring it to Iris as a present, he walked into the shop and bought the figurine.

Now I have a present for Iris, he thought, but nothing for her mother. For some reason he thought of toothpaste. That's it, he thought. Iris said her mother needed toothpaste. Stopping at the first drugstore he saw, he bought a tube of Colgate and continued his journey.

Soon he was on Market Street. The area was safe and picturesque, but several blocks up, Mission street, the neighborhood took a decided turn for the worse. Derelicts and drinkers lay in the street and garbage and wine bottles were strewn about the sidewalks. Unexpectedly, Manny began to feel paranoid. A bus went by and a little voice in the back of Manny's mind told him to catch it, and he did.

In no time at all, the bus deposited him a few blocks from Iris's apartment. As he walked up the hill, he was assailed by a familiar scent. It smelled heavy and sweet. What was it? He associated the smell with his grandmother and all at once it hit him. Irises. Irises used to grow along the side of his grandmother's house in Cambridge. Looking over his shoulder he saw a yard, and it was filled with irises. One particular flower caught his eye. He picked it and was stuffing it in his bag when he saw the naked statue with the hole where his cock should be. He plugged the hole with the stem of the flower; his present was complete.

SEVENTEEN

"Mmmmmmmmmmmmmmm . . . ." the familiar feeling hummed in his head. Manny was on the road again, but this time not alone. Randy, the other Pisces from Sourdough Sam's was with him. Randy rolled their first joint as the truck sped across the Bay Bridge on the first leg of the three thousand mile journey back East.

The week following Mury's birthday party had been a busy one. In his apartment Manny wrote several more pages of automatic writing, and in the warehouse breadmaking kits were hastily assembled and loaded onto another Rental truck. Susan and Miranda had been phoned and told of his impending visit, hopefully on Christmas Eve, and the final details of the cocaine deal were hammered out with Mury. Randy would be dropped off in Connecticut and Manny would continue the short drive over the Massachusetts line.

Manny's new traveling companion's uniform consisted of pointed cowboy boots, tan jeans, and a sweat shirt torn across the front. The supposed actor decked out in what he called his 'trucking outfit.' Also consisted of an enormous pink rose on this tee shirt. An army fatigue jacket and a pair of 'trucking gloves' with small holes across the knuckles completed which he said completed the costume.

Manny had many misgivings about traveling with Randy who struck him as a very odd character. In their first conversation together, Randy had admitted to Manny that he considered himself a totally selfish person. Manny was not so much bothered by this admission of egocentricity, as he was by the man's closed personality and air of aloofness. He was difficult to talk with and as they had to travel a great distance in close quarters. Manny had hoped to have a more pleasant companion. Nevertheless, he decided to try and build a working relationship.

Slowly he begins to draw Randy out of his shell, asking him about his acting aspirations, and how he felt about the drive across country. Manny had to be careful what he said about the trip and both he and Mury had agreed not to let Randy know about the cocaine deal.

Manny was slow to gain Randy's trust and companionship. He felt this was complicated by Randy's resentment over the fact that Mury had put Manny in charge of the trip. Trying to break down Randy's resentment, Manny told him he felt no one should be in charge, except when doing the driving, but in all other cases they were equals. Later, Manny was to regret this decision.

Randy was not the only problem Manny had to worry about. There was the question of money. Mury had given them one hundred dollars in cash and the Sourdough Sam credit card. Unfortunately, the credit; had been overextended in the push to get the one hundred thousand breadmaking kits ready for P&H Distributors, and the two men would never be able to put more than a fifteen dollar charge on the card at any one place.

In reality there was another problem facing the two truckers, but this one they were only vaguely aware of as they pushed through another snowstorm in the Sierras.

The problem was oil, or gas. The Arab states had formed something called a 'cartel'. Deciding it was time they made money from their own oil, they had raised prices and were boycotting sales to the Western Nations. California hadn't felt the gas crunch yet, but back East stations were running out of gas and there were long lines at the pumps.

There was one supply that the two men had plenty of, and that was alcohol. Before leaving California, they had stopped at several different liquor stores to avoid running over the fifteen dollar limit and having the proprietor run a credit check. Their reserve of alcohol was impressive, a bottle of one hundred proof Old Grandad bourbon, vodka, brandy, wine and several six packs, for the drive through the desert. Naturally, a supply of grass had also been laid in. They had weathered a snowstorm and made it out of the Sierras with very little trouble, and as they headed out of the mountains and into the Nevada desert, they lit another joint.

There was one area of conversation where Manny and Randy hit it off just fine, and that was on the subject of women. Driving through Reno, the two men resumed this favorite topic of conversation. Like Manny, Randy considered himself a ladies' man, but unlike Manny, he seemed to be into a sex power trip. Mury had told Manny that Randy had a size E cock and lead a pretty bizarre sex life, which included letting his friends take turns screwing his girlfriend, Jennie.

Passing through several of the small 'whore' towns in Nevada, the men had their first disagreement. Randy wanted to stop and hit a few brothels, but Manny, pressing hard to arrive home on Christmas Eve, felt they should keep on driving. Randy persisted by filling Manny in on some of his sexual escapades with his size E cock and describing the wild times he'd had when he stopped at these houses on other Sourdough Sam trips. Manny finally persuaded Randy to compromise by promising to stop on the way back west.

"Welllll, she was just seventeen, if you know what I mean, and the way she looked was way beyond compare. Oooo, I . . . The Two truckers had finally found some basis to build a relationship on, music. They each had every Beatle album that was ever produced, and as they drove through Wyoming they sang every tune. They had started to flow.

As they sang, they shared the bottle of one hundred proof Old Grandad burbon. Manny had attached the name, 'starter' to the drink, synonymously with Sourdough 'starter' of course, and wherever things began to slow down on the trip, he started them up with a quick shot.

Nearing Nebraska, Manny remembered the weigh stations. This time he knew there would be no problem as he simply planned to ignore them. If he was stopped, he would plead innocence. After all, he and Randy were only two renters who didn't know any better. Things were relaxed between the two truckers until they hit the Wyoming-Nebraska state line.

Randy insisted on stopping for gas at a station on a small bluff overlooking the highway. Manny didn't feel it was necessary as he know he had enough gas to make it well inside Nebraska. Randy, trying to re-open the old issue of who was in charge, was persistent. Manny, trying to be a nice guy and not wanting to throw his power around, give in and agreed to stop. It proved to be a mistake. Although only fifteen dollars was charged to the credit card, the service station attendant placed a call to verify the credit standing. Finding the card was well over its limit, the attendant wanted to keep the card for the twenty-five dollar bounty. Both Pisces, recognizing that if they lost the card they would be stranded, reached around the counter and grabbed the shocked attendant, shouting "Give us back that fucking card or else." He did. And Manny paid for the gas with their small cash reserve, he wondered why he hadn't listened to himself.

Driving straight on through with no stops, the two men were in Western Illinois by midnight. As Manny took his turn at the wheel, the weather turned against them. A sleet storm had blown down from the Great Lakes, and Interstate 80 was a sheet of ice. All along the highway, trucks and cars has been forced off the road. Big semi's driven by experienced truckers, jackknifed before their eyes. Manny, determined to see his family on Christmas Eve, took another shot of "starter" and kept driving. By the time he left the toll booth south of Chicago, he could do no better than thirty miles an hour on the ice slicked road.

He shifted through first, then second, and then into third with no trouble, when all at once a small Renault spun out in front of him and flew off the road like a toy car on a stereo turntable. Manny had just climber back into the cab after checking on the driver of the disabled car, when a large tractor trailer appeared out of the dark on the opposite side of the highway, and skidded on the icy pavement, crashing through the guard rail and barely missing the Rental truck. Manny ran over to see if the trucker was all right. Although shaken, he appeared to be untouched.

"Damn, I'm not letting this storm stop me," Manny told himself. He took another hit of the "starter" and steered the Rental back on the highway. Once again, he had just shifter into third when the trouble began. The rear end of the Rental began to slide to the left. Remembering his driver's training instructions, he went with the slide. As he did, the truck swung quickly to the right causing him to lose nearly all control of the vehicle. Looking up he saw the guard rail dead ahead and yelled to Randy, who was peacefully asleep in the sleeping bag. "Hoooold on," he yelled, then the truck spun around and this time he was facing the opposite guard rail. Once again he yelled, "Hoooold on." The third "Hoooold on . . ." had just begun with the Rental pulled itself out of the skid. With another shot of 'starter,' Manny managed to make it into fourth gear.

It was three a.m. before the truck stopped again. They were in Ohio and nearly out of gas. Resigned to the delay, Manny steered the truck off the highway. Very few stations were open at this hour of the morning, and some that were, has no gas. Just as Manny was about to give up, he saw a neon sign announcing, BIG JIM'S ALL NIGHT TRUCK STOP. Filling the tank to the allotted fifteen dollar limit, Randy and Manny decided to hit Big Jim's for bacon and eggs. They hadn't eaten since breakfast, and both men were starving.

Big Jim's was the epitome of the small town truck stop, complete with dumb blonde waitress snapping her gum to the music of a Country Western tune player on a small brown plastic radio perched on a dusty, corner shelf. Big Jim visible through the grill window looked mean-faced and tired. Manny figured he was probably an ex-trucker who had found his dream place. To complete the picture, three or four groups of truckers bunched together over cups of coffee as their rigs hummed outside the diner.

The two Pisces had just finished their second cup of coffee and were waiting for their check, when Randy began playing with the waitress. Something in his tone must have set her off, and instead of swooning at his ladies' man routine, she told him off. Randy, trying to save face, told her she shouldn't talk to truckers like that. At this point, the dialogue between the blonde and the world-be actor turned nasty and Manny suggested they leave. Randy paid no attention and continued his insults, but this time at a much louder volume, which attracted the attention of the other truckers. All Manny could think of was the load of commercial merchandise sitting out in the Rental and the warning the P.I.E. driver had given him on his trip west.

"They don't like scabs and would just as soon bust one's head open as look at him."

Once again, Randy told the waitress she shouldn't talk to truckers in that way, at which point she told him, staring disdainfully at his torn sweatshirt and rose-colored flower, "You may think yer' a trucker, but you sher' ain't one."

Randy's comeback was slow and deliberate. Sliding back on his stool, he placed one of his pointed cowboy boots on the counter and said in a affected Southern Drawl, "I'm not a trucker, huh? Well, I got boots like a trucker … pants like a trucker . . . gloves like a trucker," and at the top of his voice, " . . . and I sure as hell, smell like a trucker!"

Before Randy could get his boot off the counter, and the other truckers their bellies off the tables, Manny threw a five dollar bill down, grabbed Randy by the shoulders, lifting him off his stool, and shoved him through the door. As they ran to the truck and jumped inside, they began to laugh. They were still laughing when BIG JIM's was just a speck in the rearview mirror.

It was the morning of Christmas Eve and Manny couldn't see why he wouldn't be walking through Susan's door and greeting his children by nightfall. They rolled into Pennsylvania at noon and noticed a phone at the gas station where they stopped to put the usual fifteen dollars worth of gas in the truck, he decided to call Susan and let her know he would soon be home. The reception was not what he'd expected.

"Hi, Luv. It's me."

"Where are you?"

"Somewhere in Pennsylvania. I should be at your house sometime tonight."

"Well, I'm not going to be there. I'm going to my father's tonight, and the kids and I are staying until tomorrow."

"But I told you I'd be home tonight."

"Sorry, if you want to see us, you'll just have to come to my father's."

"Carrumba! Come to your father's?" Manny hadn't seen his in-laws in the two years since he and Susan had separated. Like most parents, they felt their own offspring was the party most wronged and any and all fault must lie with the other party. Manny didn't know if he could face them. "Okay, I'll see you there." He slammed the phone down and headed for the Rental.

They were driving on the interstate in New York, when Manny suggested they remain on I 80 until they reached the Mass Pike. And then drop down to Connecticut where Randy lived. He told Randy he felt they'd have more luck finding gas on the Pike on a holiday. Randy, who was now driving, ignored the suggestion and elected to follow his own route through Pennsylvania. It was nearing Christmas Eve when the truck ran out of gas on a deserted stretch of highway. The two men, barely speaking by this time, hitched to the closest rest area and called the state police to find out where to buy gas. From the police they learned a man in the next town would drive out with a can of gas for the meager sum of forty-five dollars.

A little while later the man drove up and gave them a five gallon can of gas, assuring them it would be enough to get to the next gas station. Unfortunately, the next gas station was closed for the holiday. Soon, they saw a motel sign and decided it would be impossible to make it home that night. They elected to try for a restful night's sleep.

Christmas morning, Manny was awakened by sunlight streaming through the motel window. H hadn't slept well the night before. Anxiety about his meeting with Susan's father and the forthcoming meeting with Al and his possible Mafia connections had kept him tossing and turning. Randy, for once offering a sensible suggestion, said he thought it would be better to skip breakfast and not run the credit card too high and risk a credit check.

Luck was on their side as the motel clerk was in a cheerful Christmas mood and too preoccupied to bother calling Master Charge. Breathing a sigh of relief, the two truckers pointed the Rental in the direction the clerk had told them they might find gas. Fifteen minutes later they pulled into Hoagerty, Pennsylvania, and found the only open gas pumps were in front of Seven Eleven.

Manny went into the store in search of an attendant. "Hi, I'd like some gas."

"Sorry fella', we've been out of gas since some time yesterday. Things getting' pretty tight around here."

"Maybe there's a few drops left in the hoses." Manny refused to give up so close to home.

"Go ahead and try if you want. I'll turn the pumps on, but several people have already tried that today and I'm tellin' ya, there ain't no gas."

Randy unscrewed the gas cap while Manny tried the hose marked REGULAR. Crossing his fingers, he stuck the nozzle in the empty tank and squeezed the trigger. Nothing happened. He squeezed once more, but still no gas.

"Fuck it, Manny. We're just not going to make it home today," Randy told him.

Manny couldn't give up. "Let me try the HIGH TEST." He crossed his fingers and went through the whole procedure again. First, a few drops slid sown the nozzle, then a trickle, and finally a whooshing sound was heard as a gush of gas poured from the pump. The Ryder had gas.

The clerk was astounded. "I know there was no gas. I tried it myself."

As the two men climbed into the cab for the last leg of their journey home, Manny noticed a car pulling up to the mysterious pump followed by a long line of cars. The driver looked pleased as he merrily filled his tank.

The ride from the SEVEN ELEVEN to the final destination was nothing. A mere hop to Connecticut to drop off Randy, a swift skip to the Mass Pike, and finally a jump to Route 495, and only thirty miles to go. Then twenty, then ten . . . five, four, three, two . . . one.

"Daddy's home! Daddy's home!"

EIGHTEEN

Tensions were high that Christmas Day at Susan's father's house and after opening the presents, Manny, Susan and the kids made a fast exit. From there, they went to visit Manny's family, but the reception wasn't much warmer. Although everyone was happy to see Manny, they couldn't understand how he could have left his wife and kids to run off to California to write a book. No one mentioned or thought of the fact that Susan and Manny had already been separated for two years, not that Susan had been financially independent since Manny had been laid off his sheet metal job the previous July. Manny felt from their insinuations that they didn't understand his new lifestyle and weren't likely to.

The exhausted ex-couple arrived at Susan's apartment late that night after having stopped at Bedford Farms so Manny could drop off the Rental and have a look around the place. The house, corral and woods looked fine, but there was one item missing. Manny's beautiful green 'Sports Satellite' car no longer sat in the driveway. It had been located by the finance company at Manny's brother's house and repossessed. During his absence the telephone has been disconnected and now it appeared as if the farm itself would have to be put up for sale. Manny had offered the farm to both his brother and brother-in-law in return for what he still owed on it, but both had refused the offer. He hated to let the farm go, as he had really loved the place, but felt it was impossible to come up with the money for the mortgage payments. Somewhere in the back of his mind, he hoped the dope deal would save the house at the last moment.

Before falling asleep that night, Manny and Susan made love, but the feelings between them weren't very warm. He knew she felt abandoned at his abrupt departure west and also angry and resentful that he could no longer support her and the children. He could think of nothing to say to offer her hope that the situation would change. He knew he had to stay in San Francisco and finish his book and he didn't want to tell her about possible money from a cocaine deal as it would only cause her anxiety. Trying to cheer her up Manny related the beauty of San Francisco and how pleased he was with the progress of his book, but that only served to make matters worse. He could feel there was still love for him in Susan, and he knew he cared very much about her, but their reunion had been a trying one. As he turned over, the old familiar 'hmmmm' raced through his head.

The next morning, Manny took his children with him to the Sourdough East building. His old friend Lenny was waiting for him with the hundred dollars for the return trip. The Ryder was quickly unloaded and then re-loaded, and Manny watched with pride as his four-year old son handed him boxes from the rear of the truck so he could "shummm" them down the metal rollers. On the way home, Manny stopped and bought his family cupcakes and cola which they happily shared as they drove back to Susan's, singing all the way. Spending the morning with them, he felt the old longing to be close to them and Susan, but quickly hardened his heart. Nothing could interfere with his book and a chance to save the world.

Miranda was next on his agenda. Earlier that day he had called to see if she could get away to see him and had been told her husband, William, was coming home from work early to pack for a business trip he would take the next day. The lover's reunion was moved to the following day after the meeting Manny had arranged with Al Silva.

The next morning things began badly for Manny. He had a hard time starting Susan's VW and by the time he finally arrived at the offices of Liquidated Fiduciary Unlimited, Al had already left. Manny jotted down a number where he could be reached and headed back north for his meeting with Miranda.

Once again, things didn't go smoothly. Pulling his car into the Bedford Farms Shopping Plaza parking lot, their usual meeting place, Manny saw that Miranda was not alone. For one reason or another, her babysitter hadn't shown up and Miranda had her two small daughters in tow. Since no one had eaten lunch, they decided to find some small restaurant in an out of the way place where neither would be seen together. Manny felt the fewer people who knew he was in town, the fewer questions he would have to answer. Just as they were settling into a booth, who should walk in but Bob, the gaffer from the movie set. Greetings were exchanged and Bob soon joined the group for lunch. Between conversations about the people from the movie set and bites of hamburger, Manny and Miranda exchanged quiet passionate glances. The afternoon ended with Miranda telling Manny the latest gossip concerning the Bedford Farms theatrical group and soon it was time to go. Relieved that he and Miranda hadn't changed their feeling for one another, and secure in seeing that his world hadn't crumbled during his absence, the two lovers reluctantly parted. There could be no good-bye kisses or passionate embraces until later, when the children were tucked in bed.

Back at Susan's all was quiet. The children were outside playing in the snow, and Susan was upstairs sewing. Manny headed straight for the phone and rapidly dialed the number Al's secretary had given him.

"Hello? Could I please speak with Al Silva?"

"Hang on a minute." In the background Manny could hear low conversations against a backdrop of clinking glasses and soft music. Soon, a familiar voice came on the line.

"Al here."

"Hi, Al. It's Manny."

"Manny! What happened to you this morning? My secretary said I just missed you."

"Car trouble. You know how those things are."

"Yeah, that's too bad. Well, are we going to have a chance to try it again?"

"Yes. When's the best time for you?"

"Let me see . . . today. I can't do anything. How about tomorrow, Saturday? My office will be closed but we can meet at a restaurant in Watertown called Iago's. It's right on Main Street, so you can't miss it. Could you make it at noon?"

"Sure. Noon is fine. I'd like to get this settled as soon as possible. I have to travel back to San Francisco on Monday."

"I'll see you noontime tomorrow, then. Bye."

That night Manny fell asleep in Miranda's arms on the sofa in her living room. The next morning he awoke to the sound of a little girl's voice asking, "Who was the man on the sofa?"

Full of mother's guilt, Miranda scurried the little girl back upstairs and pulled on her robe. Neither she nor Manny could believe that she had insisted he spend the night. Angry at herself for letting passion affect her better judgment and duty as a mother, Miranda quickly folded up the sofa bed and made some coffee. Watching her move about the kitchen, Manny felt perhaps he should have insisted on going home, but felt that last night he needed not only a rest, but to held by someone who could understand his need to write and the desire for fame. He and Miranda shared that desire to do more than simply exist. Like him, she has a spouse and family who couldn't relate to her desires to be an actress and felt actors and writers were always other people; people who only existed on television or in fairy books.

As he pulled out of her driveway, Manny could feel some of his strength return. The night with Miranda had done him good and the hmmmm . . . feeling in his head was nearly gone. The big meeting with cousin Al was scheduled for the next morning, and Manny wanted to be in good shape.

*   *   *

Tooling down Route 128 in Susan's orange VW wagon, Manny felt better than he had expected. Surprisingly, he wasn't nervous. But the winter sun reflected off the white snow hit the windshield and hurt his eyes. He took the dark sunglasses off the dashboard and slipped them on. Gone was the tension of the past several weeks. His mind seemed to slip into automatic pilot. He knew exactly what had to be done, and he was confident he could do it. All that was required was a mechanical ability to take one step at a time, similar to unloading and re-loading the truck.

As he entered Watertown, Manny looked for a sign announcing the restaurant. He wasn't sure where the place was but knew that if it was on Main Street, it couldn't be far.

"Iago . . . Iago," he repeated out loud. The name had been running around his head since Al had told him the name of the meeting place. Just as he remembered that Iago was the name of Shakespeare's arch villain, Manny saw the sign on his left. Parking the car, Manny repeated the name once more.

"Iago ." It seemed to have an ominous ring.

Walking from the bright noontime sun into the restaurant, it seemed to Manny as if night had suddenly descended. The restaurant was dark and sparsely populated. He paused for a moment, trying to allow his eyes to adjust to the sudden change, and then proceeded into the area marked, LOUNGE.

As he sauntered up to the bar, he observed several men wearing turtleneck shirts, fedoras and dark sunglasses. Manny had seen every gangster movie ever made and if this was a mob hangout, he knew he looked as if he fit right in. Except for the fedora, his outfit matched everyone else's.

Well, he thought to himself. If I have any acting talent at all, I'd better start using it.

Motioning the bartender over, he adopted a gruff but cool tone. "Gimme' a Grandad on the rocks." Waiting for his drink, he casually glanced around the room hoping to catch a glimpse of Al. He noticed a few more people in the back seated at the tables and in the booths but couldn't recognize Al among them. The old jukebox and the dim lighting combined to give the place a sinister atmosphere.

A man wearing an overcoat and fedora took a seat at the bar and broke the silence by ordering a drink. Manny notice his own glass was empty and called to the bartender for another. Soon, more people began filtering in and conversation replaced the deathly silence. Manny was surprised that there were no women in the place. As the noise and drink eased his tension, Manny struck up a conversation with a newcomer to his left. He had just remarked about the "fine weather" when he heard someone call his name.

"Hey, hey Manny." It was his cousin, Al Silva heading his way with a big grin and an outstretched hand. He was flanked by two rough looking characters who were introduced as business associated. Coolly and calmly Manny acknowledged the greeting and introductions.

Al made an excuse to the two men that he wanted to talk to his cousin in private, and Manny acting as if he did this every day, followed him to a corner booth. As soon as they were seated, a waitress appeared out of nowhere and Al ordered scotch and water and Manny his usual Grandad on the rocks.

As quickly as the waitress appeared with their drinks, the smile disappeared from, Al's face. Watching him over the rim of his glass, Manny wondered if it was fear he saw in Al's eyes, or worry, or both.

Suddenly the fear was replaced by a smile. "Well, how are you, Manny? How was the trip?" The two men ran the gamut of small talk as they became reacquainted. Finally, Manny surreptitiously brought up the subject of the dope deal.

"Did you find anyone who might be able to handle the problem I spoke to you about on the phone?"

"Yes." Al's smile faded once again. And then, in hushed secretive tones, "How much stuff are we talking about, Manny?"

"Fifteen Pounds."

"That's a lot of snow."

"I know. How much is it worth?"

"It depends on how good it is. If it's decent, four hundred and fifty grand."

Manny, without wincing or batting an eyelash, calmly replied, "How do we do it?"

"You bring the stuff to me in Boston. I fly down to New York with a sample. If it checks out okay, right in the airport. Again, like I said, if it checks out decent, they give me the money. I fly back, and we make the exchange."

"Sounds good. But one thing, Al. Who is it that you're dealing with? Is it the Irish mafia?" There is no answer.

In the silence that followed, Manny observed the look of fear and anxiety on his cousin's face. He knew Al had been around and involved with some pretty heavy deals, and he had expected the man to behave with the coolness of a professional.

Before Al broke the silence, Manny strongly felt his fear. "Listen, Manny, this is dangerous business. People get killed for this kind of money. Be very careful, and whatever you do . . . don't go anywhere with anyone you don't know. Do you understand? Not anyone!" Manny only nodded.

With the business deal concluded, his older cousin flashed a smile. Reaching in his pocket, he handed Manny a small tinfoil packet.

"What's this?"

"Just a little cocaine to help smooth out the road on your trip back West." Manny thanked him and the two shook hands and parted.

Back out in the sunlight, Manny breathed a sigh of relief. This part was over.

NINETEEN

The Route 495 signs were replaced by Mass Pike signs as Manny headed down to Connecticut to pick up Randy for the drive back west. As he drove, his mind reviewed the last few days. He had accomplished most of his major objectives, but had to admit his visit had not been one of the most enjoyable in his life.

That last night with Miranda had almost ended in disaster. They had gone out for drinks and Chinese food and by the time they reached Manny's farm for their' farewell, the combination of bourbon, chicken chow mien, and nerves had sent Manny running to the bathroom. He would no sooner quell the spasms of nausea that racked his body and hightail it back under the sheets with Miranda, where he hoped to replace the nauseous feeling with spasms of orgasm. Unfortunately only fresh waves of illness would hit him and he would have to run back to the bathroom. To top it off, he had broken down and told Miranda about the dope deal and ended up feeling guilty for having worried her on their last night together. Being vulnerable, he also broke down and asked Miranda to leave her husband and children and come back to San Francisco with him. She almost agreed, but as the lovemaking subsided and the night ended, they both realized the whole thing was impossible. The brief flicker of hope they shared was quickly extinguished, and the pain of parting was only that much more difficult.

The last day with Susan had been even worse. Along with Manny's brothers and sisters, Susan had driven out to the farm to help him pack some of his personal belongings onto the Rental. Susan calmly watched as Manny's clothes, record albums, collection of toy soldiers, waterbed, some furniture and odds and ends were loaded onto the truck. It wasn't until Manny went to take down the lavabo, a wooden wall planter which hung on the living room wall, when all hell broke loose. The planter had been a wedding present to the young couple, and Susan refused to let him take it. In front of his family, Susan began screaming and crying and finally ran out of the house. Manny ran after her, stopping the car just as she backed out of the driveway. He didn't want to leave with bad feelings between them. He tried to calm her down by offering her anything from the house except the waterbed and his record collection. She decided to force Manny out the collection of Beatle albums. He relented and she returned with him back into the house.

Just as Manny was about to leave, his brother, David, motioned him outside. Following Dave out to the barn, Manny debated telling him about the dope deal. As the next eldest male in the family, Manny felt he would be the most logical person to know should anything go wrong. As Dave retrieved a tab of acid from the barn where he had hidden it, and offered it to Manny as a going away present, Manny decided he would tell no one else. The fewer people to worry about him, the better.

A highway sign announcing a service station at the next exit pulled Manny out of his reverie. He had read in the local paper that the 'cartel' gas crisis was getting worse, so he decided to stop not knowing what lay ahead. As it turned out, the attendant would only sell him ten gallons of gas. Manny paid, but told the kid it would be hard to get across country if he could only buy ten gallons at each station. The attendant just shrugged his shoulders. Manny started the Rental and headed back to the highway for the short trip to Randy's parents' house. As he drove, he thought about the phone call he had placed to Mury to tell him he had made the deal for four hundred and fifty thousand dollars. Mury's response was less than enthusiastic. He told Manny he was having some problem with Sourdough Sam, but refused to elaborate over the phone.

Randy's parents talked Manny into staying for dinner. After coffee and desert, the two men loaded Randy's possessions onto the Rental. Randy had decided to bring along his stamp and coin collection, dresser, two suitcases, and two rifles which they tucked away under the seat of the Rental's cab. He also insisted on bringing a live hand grenade. Manny wasn't thrilled about carrying the grenade on the long trip, but relented in the end. He had handled them in the army and knew they were pretty safe, as long as their pin wasn't pulled. Besides, if they ran into any hostile truckers, they would be ready.

Randy also had a contribution for the 'dope' stash. Friends of his had given him more pot and several different types of speed. To this they added another bottle of one hundred proof Grandad, a pint of cherry flavored Vodka, and a gallon of red 'truckin' wine.

Finally, they were ready to roll. Armed with the hundred dollars cash from Lenny, the bogus credit card from Sourdough Sam's and a dozen tuna and egg sandwiches from Randy's mother, the two truckers started their journey. It was Monday night, which meant they wouldn't arrive at Eastern Stoneware to pick up the batch of cheese crocks until New Year's Eve, barring any unforeseen calamities, that is.

Except for a few problems finding gas, the ride to Illinois and been uneventful. It was eight o'clock on New Year's Eve when the two men pulled their truck into the Eastern Stoneware parking lot. As they made their way to the loading dock, Manny noticed a thermometer on the side of the building. It registered two degrees below zero. The Midwest was being hit by one of its cold 'Canadian High' spells. The two men had expected to hastily pick up the load, and share a few drinks in some warm cozy bar before resuming their trip West. Their expectations proved to be way off.

Searching the building, they found it nearly empty. Finally, Manny found the man who was temporarily in charge of the loading platform. He told the two men that their load of crocks couldn't be released until shipping invoice was personally signed by J. Horner, himself. Manny couldn't figure out why Horner would have to sign a routine invoice to release an order of cheese crocks. After arguing with the surly shipper for a few minutes, Randy and Manny gave up. They had no choice but to wait for Jack Horner.

At ten o'clock, the tired and cold truckers finally got word that Horner had been located at a party, and world be over when he could get away. Hot coffee with a shot of 'starter' helped ease the waiting and fend off the cold. They were just about to pour their third shot, when Manny was shocked out of his numbness by an angry familiar voice.

"Where the fuck is my hundred dollars?" Horner's face was a torrid red, as he approached from the warehouse. "Lenny says you have hundred dollars for me!"

"That's the first I heard of it." Manny was truly surprised. "I don't even know what hundred dollars you're talking about. I'm only the truck driver."

"I'm talking about the hundred dollars I lent you the last time you were here. That came out of my personal checking account, and Sourdough Sam was supposed to reimburse me. Now, I'm not releasing this load until I get my money."

Manny tried to calm the angry salesman. "Look, I don't know anything about your money. I figured you got that a long time ago. There's nothing I can do about it. I don't even have a hundred dollar."

"I'm not releasing the load until I get my money." Replied Horner, this time slightly less adamant.

Manny's first suggestion was that he contact Lenny Solens. Unfortunately, Lenny wasn't home. Then it hit him, Mury! He knew Mury could handle Horner, even two thousand miles away, and he was right. A smiling salesman hung up the phone. As Manny had hoped, Mury had smoothed over the situation by promising to send a money gram right after the holidays. Jack Horner signed the invoice and wished them a 'Happy New Year'.

The Canadian cold front had infiltrated the entire Midwest and it was still below zero as the yellow Rental drove through the mountains of Wyoming. Manny drove as Randy slept. He alternated between taking swigs of the 'trucking' wine and scraping the ice from the windshield. He had only six square inches of clear viewing, and the truck would do only twenty-five miles an hour, uphill or down. Manny hadn't seen another vehicle since Cheyenne, and he was worried. He knew if the truck stalled, there was a good chance they would freeze to death.

By morning, they were out of the mountains. As Manny pulled into a gas station, the bright sun shone over the plains. He asked the attendant what the temperature was, and was shocked to learn, that even with the bright sunshine, it was thirty below zero. Involuntarily, he shivered as he thought of the night in the mountains. To celebrate his triumph over the cold and ice, Manny broke off half the acid crystal his brother had given him. With Randy still sound asleep Manny headed west.

Manny's second acid 'trip' proved to be a totally different experience from the one on the night of Mury's birthday party. Driving along he saw a man stop his car on a mountain to his right only a short distance away. The man got out of his car and walked down the side of the mountain to a drainage pipe and began to dig with shovel. Thinking that was odd, Manny laughed so loud he woke Randy and pointed to the man on the hill. Randy looking up saw nothing and cursed Manny for waking him, but three miles down the road and astounded, Randy pointed up at the mountain. Just coming into view was a man with a shovel digging around a drainage ditch. Manny had had telescopic vision. This time both men laughed wildly.

Pulling into a truck stop for gas and lunch, Manny was hit by still more visual effects from the acid. While they were eating dinner, his food flew off his plate and the room bent in odd shapes. In the washroom, preparing to shave, Manny looked in the mirror and watched in amazement as his half-shaven chin stretched and moved to the left, causing him to look as if he had an L-shaped head. Unperturbed, Manny simply shaved the 'L'.

As they left the 'Little America' truck stop, Manny dozed while Randy took his turn at the wheel. In what seemed to be no time at all, Manny awoke and found the truck setting on the side of the highway somewhere in the middle of the Great Salt Lake Desert. Randy had run out of gas. Fortunately, this trip they had thought to carry a can of gas with them, and the extra five gallons carried them to a Nevada filling station. The instant they pulled away from the station, Randy reminded Manny of his promise to stop in one of the 'Little Reno' whore towns." Anxious to keep pushing to San Francisco, Manny nevertheless, kept his promise, and soon the two were stopping in a town called Elko, Nevada.

Randy announced it was 'fun and games' time and the two Pisces split all of the of the remaining acid, snorted Al's cocaine and finished up with a joint before setting out on the streets of Elko to pursue their desires.

Elko had five whorehouses, and all were on one street sitting side by side. Each house look identical and the only differentiating marks were the signs: SUE'S S&M, LIL'S P&G, and so forth. The two eager truckers tried several establishments, but for some reason were only granted admittance to one, PAM's B&D.

Pam, herself, led the truckers to a western style bar where two sheepherders were quietly drinking a beer at the far end of the long saloon.

Drinks were ordered, and the two men were introduced to a darkly, dressed woman named Trina. Her first question was the standard one.

"What are a couple of good looking dudes like you boys doing out all alone?"

Formalities over, Randy and Manny argued over who would get the pretty woman. Finally, it was decided that Trina would go to bed with both of them, seeing they were such good 'trucking buddies'.

Trina had difficulty arranging herself so she could make love to two men simultaneously, so Manny stepped in to orchestrate. Randy was instructed to lie on his back so Trina could suck his huge cock, while Manny screwed her from behind. After fifteen minutes of rollicking, lovemaking, and shifting positions, Manny had cum. Slipping out of the room, so as not to disturb Randy, who seemed to be having trouble getting off, Manny headed for the bar for another drink.

Setting at the bar waiting for Randy, Manny met a striking black girl named Loreen. She invited him up to her room for a 'good time', but Manny explained he had just had a 'goodtime' with one of her girlfriends. The two ordered another round of drinks and started dancing. One thing led to another, and soon Manny found himself back upstairs. By this time, the combination of drugs and alcohol was really taking hold. Soon Manny began 'whooping' and 'hollering' and found himself dancing on top of the bed with the charming Loreen. Their reverie was interrupted by the Madam who, entering the room without knocking, informed Manny that his friend needed more money as he still hadn't relieved himself. Manny streaked down the hall stark naked with money he had borrowed from Randy as the Madam followed in hot pursuit.

"This here is a respectable joint." Admonishing Manny.

It was nearly five a.m. when Manny hauled the unconscious Randy into the truck. As he started the ignition, he saw the gas gauge was nearly on empty. Just then, Randy rolled over and got his head stuck between the seat and the gear shift. Manny finally freed his head and started the search for the elusive petrol. As he drove through the streets of Elko, Manny recalled Randy telling him the town would be full of gas stations. As usual, Randy was wrong. Manny finally just made it to an open station twenty miles down the road.

The sun was shining brightly as the 'daring duo', their new name for themselves, stopped the Rental in the Sierra Nevada's to pick up a huge snowball to bring to San Francisco. The mountains were the last obstacle between them and the safety of Sourdough Sam's. All they had to do was push over the top of the mountains and sail down the other side to the coast. However, first they had to get over the top and that proved to be tough going. The Rental had been pushed full throttle the entire trip, and it was beginning to slow sown. On the smaller inclines, the engine would only do fifteen miles per hour and on the steeper grades, only five. As they climbed up one particularly steep mountain road, Manny could barely get the tired truck moving at all. Following a sign marked SCENIC OVERLOOK; Manny pulled the truck over to give it a rest.

As the two men smoked a joint and sipped 'starter', Manny had an idea. Getting out of the cab, he opened the hood of the truck. The engine was quiet, but appeared to be in great pain. Removing the cap from the bottle of Old Grandad, Manny whispered a few words of encouragement and ceremoniously poured a good dose of the brown liquid over the engine. The heat radiating from the motor was so hot; the bourbon appeared to be absorbed right into the cast iron. Manny gingerly closed the hood and ran around to the side of the truck where he repeated his ritual. The gas cap was removed, more words of encouragement spoken, and a generous amount of the 'starter' was poured into the gas tank. With a healthy shot for himself, Manny quickly got behind the wheel of the Rental.

The engine started right and purred softly. Realizing that the steepest hills were still to come, Manny gently put her in first gear. The truck began to move. First five miles per hour . . . then ten . . . fifteen into second gear. Gathering steam, Manny shifter into third. Thirty-five miles per hour . . . the truck was moving, now. They passed other trucks and cars, and soon they were well into fourth and still climbing. Fifty miles per hour and they were hitting the top of the mountain.

"We're truckin'!" Manny screamed as the truck rocked down the hill at eighty and ninety.

"San Francisco, here we come!!"

TWENTY

The two Pisces swaggered through Sourdough's door unshaven, in dirty clothes and brandishing rifles under their arms.

"You all lookin' fer a couple a 'truckers?'"

The joke was perfect. Mury didn't recognize either of them, not even Manny who had a wide brimmed hat pulled down over his face and his pants tucked into the 'trucking' boots he had brought from home. Everyone laughed. Work was ceased, champagne corks popped, and joints were lit. A snowman, built from the huge snowball the truckers had brought from the mountains, was placed in front of Sourdough Sam's in the warm California sun. Manny felt good to be back to the 'safe rock'.

When the celebrating died down to a reasonable roar, Manny was introduced to a man quietly setting in the special rocker. He was Dr. Heinrich Von Stuben, or Dr. Hank, as Mury called him. While Manny turned to tell Margo some of the trucking exploits, Dr. Hank took Mury in a corner to talk about some business. Manny couldn't overhear, but he could tell that Mury was wearing a forced smile. Something was wrong back at Sourdough Sam's.

Later, after dinner and drinks, Manny found out what the trouble was. Mury told him that Dr. Hank was a lawyer working for Speningers, the people they bought pans from. He was also working hand in hand with P&H Company, who had a grievance with Sourdough Sam's' Mury glossed over exactly what the grievance was. At any rate, a lot of money was owed, and Dr. Hank had been sent to get it.

Fortunately for Sourdough Sam's, Mury, with his gift of gab and Manny at his side for support, managed to persuade Dr. Von Stuben not to sue the company at this time. Dr. Hank seemed impressed with Mury and had stated that for the most part, he was on his side. This caused Mury to take heart because among other things, Dr. Von Stuben was the president and founder of a large profit making college at Lake Tahoe, and one of the better known lawyers in that part of the country. He was a good person to have on their side, even if he did travel around with a non-car-trained dog in the back seat of his little Datsun.

When they were alone, the conversation finally turned to the dope deal. Manny related all the details of the trip east, including his relationship with Mury's friend Randy. Things had gone better on the return trip, and Manny thought that they had built up a good rapport until the last fifty miles. At that point, Randy wanted to stop to eat, but Manny said that he thought it didn't make any sense with them being so close to their destination. After their last gas stop, Randy jumped into the driver's side of the Rental and had insisted on driving. Manny, again playing the nice guy, relented. At the first hamburger place they came to, Randy stopped and ate. Manny didn't, nor did he speak to his Pisces brother for the rest of the journey.

Mury listened to the writer's narrative quietly with only a nod here and there. When Manny finished, Mury stated: "I'm going to make the next trip back east," implying he would make the final dope connection.

"I doubt that my connection will buy that, Mury."

"They'll buy it, because we have the merchandise," Mury assured him. Then added: "We're going to have to 'beat the bushes' in order to come up with the last ten of the twenty-five thousand we need to make the cocaine buy."

"What so you mean?"

"When I gave Rocket the third five thousand dollar installment to get the deal on the way, the bank called Jack Sterns the treasurer of Sourdough Sam's. He in turn called me, and I was only able to convince him to okay the check by explaining that we were diversifying into the jewelry business. I told him the money was a down payment for gems we were getting from Rocket, but I don't dare try for any more money from Sourdough Sam's"

"How are we going to get the rest of the money?"

"Probably by getting a third party to buy into the cocaine deal for a percentage."

This last statement worried Manny who remembered Al's words about not talking to anyone you didn't know.

*　　*　　*

The next day Manny tried to get back to his writing. He worked all day, but by the afternoon he still had nothing on paper; not even automatic writing. Around four he gave up and decided to visit Sourdough Sam's for a little inspiration from Mury. By now, the dope deal was beginning to consume all his waking hours.

At Sam's Mury told Manny that he and Bobby were going to leave on an excursion East in a few days. Manny had arranged a meeting in Chicago with a man who might want to buy into the cocaine deal. From Chicago they would travel to Boston via Amtrak, as Mury was planning a little honeymoon for him and Bobby who hadn't had much time together lately.

Mury, Manny, and Bobby had just decided to go out to dinner when Jennie, Randy's girlfriend, stopped by. She was upset, informing the trio that Randy had called after his trip to tell her he didn't think he wanted to see her anymore. Murray invited her along to dinner as a consolation. After dinner, Jennie invited Manny back to her house for more consolation.

Needless to say, the consolation took place on Jennie's king-sized water bed. Manny found her to be warm and sensitive, but a bit on the flaky side. She played a Rod McKuen poetry album as they made love.

Her love making reminded Manny of another Aries lover he had known just before the trip to San Francisco. She also liked to fuck, fuck, fuck, rapidly until the wee hours. So Manny fuck, fuck, fucked, Jennie, until she screamed.

TWENTY-ONE

"I'm sorry, Mr. Nestor is away on business and won't be back for three or four weeks. May I take a message?"

"No. I'll call again."

Mury, who had been gone nearly a week, had left Manny in charge of the Sourdough Sam operation. This way messages from Rocket, who was south of the border trying to buy the cocaine, and Mury, who was frantically scouring the East Coast for another ten grand, could be taken by Manny and relayed back and forth without some strange person becoming suspicious. As he hung up the phone and busied himself with some paperwork, Manny wondered how Mury and his lover, Bobby, were getting along. He knew they must be in Boston by now, and he hoped their love relationship was running smoothly.

Manny didn't understand the nature of the difficulty between the two men, but he was glad he'd had the opportunity to observe a homosexual relationship firsthand. The night before Bobby and Mury left for the trip East, Manny and Iris had joined them for dinner. As the evening progressed, Manny could feel the same love coming from Mury towards Bobby, as he himself felt for Iris. He now felt certain that homosexual relationships were no threat to mankind and were similar to heterosexual relationships. After all, love was love.

Later that night, Iris and Manny decided to sleep on Mury's couch rather that drive home at an ungodly hour. As the two lay on the sofa bed, they decided to add spark of life to Mury and Bobby's evening. They waited until there was no noise coming from the bedroom and then put the album 'Love Unlimited' on the stereo, turning the dial up to full volume. When the needle dropped down on the record, the love theme blasted throughout the entire apartment, but particularly through the two enormous speakers that hung over Murray's dresser. Iris and Manny could hear laughter from the bedroom and soon settled down to enjoy the song themselves. Over the past few weeks, it had become their love song, too.

However the relationship between Iris and Manny was going much better than the one between the two homosexual lovers. Even Mury and Iris seemed to have found some rapport. Iris no longer viewed Manny as "that homo" who wanted to get into Manny's pants, and Mury was beginning to see that Iris wasn't nearly the ball buster he had originally labeled her. A three-way relationship had begun to evolve.

A few days after Manny had returned from Massachusetts, he and Iris had decided to give Mury a belated Christmas present. Together they planned the gift and carefully decorated it to surprise Mury. It was a five foot bottle of wine encased in a pyramid-shaped carton. They had decorated it with joints, poems, various flavored sex lubricants, and love oils. To complete the surprise, Iris and Manny exchanged clothes and roles. He dressed in her clothes, she in his. Laughing, they carried their surprise up the steps to Mury's apartment. Gail, who was just getting out of her car, helped them and soon a party was in the making.

After the wine was uncorked and consumed, Gail took Manny aside and mentioned the change that had come over Iris. She told him she had never seen Iris so mellow and happy. Manny told Gail he felt Iris was really two different people; Iris, a hard-nosed business woman, and Michelle, a soft feminine lover. Manny viewed the relationship in relation to Iris's Libran personality; when it was good, it was very, very good; and when it was bad it was horrid!"

Their relationship had been very, very good the day they drove to Salinas. Manny never spent a more beautiful day in his life. It felt like a movie. He and Iris tooled up the coast road in her little 'bug' with the scent of eucalyptus enveloping them as they drank wine from the bottle. The joint they shared seemed to smooth the day into a kaleidoscope of cliffs, ocean, and love. At the cozy little restaurant where they stopped to eat, the piano player seemed to be playing just for them.

The feelings between them had blossomed to the point where they could hardly keep their hands off each other. They kissed over drinks at funky little bars; they kissed at the movies, and not only at the romantic parts; and they kissed in Golden Gate Park in the little Japanese garden.

Manny loved Iris intensely, even though she still had her moments and could be as Mury had said, 'a ball buster.' One of those times was a day he had told her about his 'fuck-fuck-fuck' episode with Jennie. He had no idea she would react so strongly. After all, he had told her about his visit to the whorehouse in Elko, and she had thought that amusing. But the story of his brief fling with Jennie did not amuse Iris in the least. She read him the riot act and started in on Manny's relationship with Susan. She wanted him to get a divorce. Soon, they had developed a running scenario.

"I can't afford a divorce," was Manny's standard reply.

"It only costs fifty dollars in California," was Iris's comeback.

Around and around they went. Manny argued that it only cost fifty dollars if it went uncontested. A divorce would mean alimony and child support, and that world mean another routine job. No, he had to wait until his book was published. Then money would be no problem.

Thoughts of his children brought back the old feeling of longing, and the short visit at Christmas only served to make him miss them more. He fantasized having Susan send them out to California for a visit. Maybe he could use his income tax check, when and it if came, and buy two plane tickets. One fantasy led to another. If the dope deal came through he could afford to buy a small plane and fly them out himself. Or, maybe his book would be an overnight best seller and he could afford to fly his entire family to San Francisco. If, if, if, lead to thoughts of the book.

The book, the fucking book, Manny repeated to himself. He had been at Sourdough Sam's for months now, and still there was little on paper.

Okay, you asshole, get your fingers on those typewriter keys and start writing. Okay, here goes. And Manny began to type.

"Who knows, maybe something will turn up.

Heaven knows you have enough running around in your head right now. In the last few days your life has gone from heaven to hell and back. I now realize that I am feeling Mury's feelings. I have the ring on, and I realize with the ring, the wearer has an extra resistance. Like the ring gives off an invisible shield, a protective shield. The protective shield gives off positive charges of electricity which absorb the negative charges that are constantly bombarding one. Positive and negative do not necessarily mean good or bad.

Enough positive energy can be stored in an object, such as t his ring, until there is a surplus supply of positive energy which a human being can tap and use during a period of stress or personal trouble. This source of positive energy will carry a person until he can build up his own energy source again.

Even if people consider this only in someone's mind. Because it really is only in a person's mind, it is still happening. WHY ARE YOU TRYING TO WRITE, TONIGHT? YOUR HEAD IS MUSH!

Manny couldn't write another sentence. His concentration was non-existent. Something was bothering him, but he couldn't quite put his finger on what.

Atmosphere, that's it, he thought. Something strange is happening around me, here at Sourdough Sam's. But what?

It had started with Jerry Wilson. Manny could feel the man watching him with those strange cat eyes. Other people were acting strangely, too. Whenever he walked into a room, conversations ended abruptly. Even the usually friendly Ned was acting peculiar, 'fer sure'. The call Manny had received last night from Rocket didn't help put his mind at ease.

"Hello, Manny. This is Rocket."

"Hi. I've been waiting for you to call. How are things in Columbia?"

"I'm not in Columbia, but I'm almost ready to leave."

"Carrumba! You were supposed to be there a week ago! What the hell have you been doing?" Manny could hear voices in the background and it had him worried. Rocket had been instructed to work alone, except for the Columbian connection. Through the receiver, Manny could here Rocket's muffled voice.

"Shut up, Lonny!" Rocket returned to the phone. "Listen little buddy, I had a little problem. I'm going to need some more money to get things going."

"What are you talking about? Mury already laid fifteen grand on you!"

Manny recalled the night the money had been exchanged. Rocket had arrived at Sam's with another sample of cocaine, and Bobby, Mury, Manny and Rocket proceeded to get 'blasted' or 'ripped', as Rocket would say. Manny could still picture the three men standing in Mury's office, arms encircling each other, and tears running down their faces. What a night that had been.

Rocket was trying to tell Mury how much he loved him, and how he world die before he would let anything happen to his friend. At the same time, Manny was trying to break in and conduct a cocaine deal. To further complicate matters, Bobby and Mury were at a point of severe strain in their relationship, and Bobby kept trying to pull away from the group and finally succeeded which only hurt Mury who sobbed louder with his arms around Rocket. Rocket kept blubbering how much he loved Mury, and Mury trying to respond kindly, but broken up about Bobby, would alternately blubber about how much he loved Rocket, too, cr . . . he was having so many hassles with Bobby and this cocaine deal, but . . . he was convinced the deal was a righteous one and things would work out in the end.

Manny, standing on the sidelines and trying to figure out what was going on, finally had to intervene with a firm, "What the hell is going on here! Is this a love in or a business deal?" As he had hoped, his command broke up the circle of tears and professions of love. "Now, let's go into the living room and get this business over with."

Soon everyone was calm, and as they passed around a joint, an animated conversation began. Manny told Rocket how he had foreseen the cocaine deal before it had ever begun. He mentioned the day he had met Rocket and had told Mury a man was outside who wanted to see him. For some reason, Mury denied ever having had the conversation. Manny was shocked. He and Mury had never miscued and Manny wondered if Mury had forgotten, or if he didn't want Rocket to know he had prior knowledge of the deal. An uncomfortable silence followed.

Glancing at Rocket out of the corner of his eye, Manny could sense the man's fear. For the first time he had seen a discrepancy in Manny and Mury's story. A few minutes later, Rocket asked to see Manny in the other room, "in private."

"There's something important I have to know about you, little buddy."

"What is it?"

"I know you told me had heavy family connections and all, but if you do, how come you have blue eyes? Shouldn't they be brown?"

"I have some English blood. Half my family has blue eyes, and half brown eyes. It's not uncommon. Is that all you called me in here for?" Manny tried to make it as light as possible.

"Yah, except for one more thing. I want you to know you never have to worry if you're out with me. I will protect you. You never have to be afraid of anything. I would kill anyone who put a finger on you."

Thanks for the offer Rocket, but I'm not afraid of much. I can handle myself pretty well." Manny patted the side of his pants to indicate a gun. Rocket seemed impressed.

Manny was then brought back to the present by more muffled voices on the telephone line and another, "Shut up!" It seemed to him as if Rocket was even more paranoid and crazy than before. In a flash, the familiar voice was back on the line.

"I need money, little buddy." Manny was silent for a moment trying to decide what he should say.

"There's nothing I can do about the money right now, Rocket. You'll have to do the best you can with what you have."

"I'll try," was Rocket's disappointed reply. "There's one more thing, though. I want to bring the jewels straight to Sourdough's when I get back in the country."

Jewel was the code word for cocaine, and Manny replied quickly. "No way! We don't want you within a hundred miles of this place. When you get back to the States, call. We'll tell you what to do, then."

Actually, neither Mury nor Manny had decided how to handle the delivery of the cocaine, but Manny wanted to calm Rocket down and give him the impression that things were running smoothly. Rocket seemed appeased and told Manny he would call again.

The entire conversation left Manny feeling uneasy. He wondered what the hell Rocket had done with the money Mury had given him, and who this fellow, Lonny was. He tried to reach Mury to let him know about the newest developments, but no one answered the phone at the hotel. His stomach was churning, and he could feel a burning sensation in his throat. The deal was getting heavy, and Manny's body was reacting to the stress.

The writer-turned-manager had no idea what time it was when he finally drifter off to sleep that night, but he knew he heard footsteps moving back and forth, like pacing, in Sourdough Sam's apartment across the hall. The next morning, he woke with a pounding headache. He stumbled into the bathroom, put in his lenses, and immediately downed three aspirins and two of Mury's Vitamin 'C's'. He made his way down to the warehouse and headed for the coffee pot. Just as he was about to add the sugar, Jerry Wilson and Jack Sterns, the treasurer of Sourdough Sam's, rounded the corner and headed for the door. Neither man spoke to Manny. Something was up.

Ned arrived and informed Manny that Sourdough Sam, himself, was back in town. Those footsteps Manny had heard last night weren't part of a dream. The two men talked over coffee and soon, Jerry returned and asked where the rubber stamp with Sourdough Sam's name on it was kept. He said the treasurer needed it and also some papers from the safe. Now, Manny knew without a doubt, that trouble was in the air. He had to get out of the office and try to figure out what to do. He went back upstairs to Murray's apartment and sat on the couch smoking a joint.

The last puff of smoke was curling from his mouth as he turned and looked out the bay window. The school across the street looked ancient. It was a large stucco structure with cracks running down each side. Manny could see kids playing in a yard further down the block. As he watched the tranquil scene, he could feel the smoke taking effect. Unfortunately, it didn't seem to ease the churning in his stomach. His gaze returned to the school, and it was then he saw the man. He was wearing a business suit and had on a hat. He stood directly in front of a parked car reading a newspaper. Manny hadn't seen many people dressed like that in this area before. He rose and walked to the window for a better look. He froze. There was another man. He, too, was dressed in a suit. As he leaned lazily against a parked car, his eyes seemed focused on Sourdough Sam's Warehouse.

Jesus, it's the narks', he thought. Manny tried to figure out what to do next. They must be watching the warehouse.

Manny's mind whirled in panic. Get your stuff quick and get the hell out of here, he said to himself. Fuck the cocaine! You don't want to go to jail.

He began to pace and suddenly a bizarre thought occurred to him. H could write in jail.

He returned to the window for another look. Suddenly the men looked more like mafia 'hit' men. "Call Mury," Manny said out loud to no one. "That's the best thing to do. Then, get out." He returned to the window and was more convinced than ever that the men were watching. He moved back from the window, wondering how long they had been out there. His mind began to race. What if he called Mury and the phones were 'bugged'? He returned to the window just as one of the men got into his car. He didn't pull away, he just sat there. That clinched it for Manny. Definitely, the men were narks.

"Rrrrrrriiiiiinnnnnngggggg . . . . . . !" The school bell was ringing and kids were running out of school and fanning out in all directions. A little girl approached the first 'nark' and got into his car. The car pulled away. A little boy ran to the next car, and soon they too pulled away.

You fucking asshole, Manny thought to himself, you're just stoned and paranoid. Nothing is wrong. In the next instant Manny thought about this morning's events at the warehouse, and Jerry Wilson and the treasurer. Something had to be wrong. He had never trusted Jerry. What if somehow they had found out about the dope deal and told Sourdough Sam? What if they had called the narks? Manny decided he had to call Mury, but not from the phone in the apartment. He would walk down to the phone near the Save More.

*   *   *

"Listen, Mury, I'm telling you, something funny is going on out here. I can't quite put my finger on what, but I can feel something is wrong."

"Come on, Manny. Get a hold of yourself. You're just getting cold feet because the deal is about to come down."

"What do you mean?"

"Your old buddy Lenny has things all worked out for us. He made a deal to sell a sample of the jewels for a grand. We're making the transaction tonight at the Marriot. If there people like our stuff, they might put up the extra ten thousand we need. So stop worrying, things couldn't be better. Lenny's really pleased about the deal. He told me it would help him settle an old family debt. Wait a sec', Lenny wants to say hello."

"Hi Manny. I hear things are going pretty good for you out in San Francisco."

"Yah, things are pretty nice out here. How's Flo?"

"She's doing fine. She's on vacation in Bermuda. Listen Manny, don't worry about the deal. Everything is fine. Like Mury told you, I'm glad to do my part 'cause it will help me settle an old family vendetta."

"Sounds good to me."

"Hey, I might see you in a month or so. I hope to get out to San Francisco, myself. If not, you have a good time. Here's Mury again."

"Listen you crazy fucking Portagee,' there's nothing to worry about, especially with Rocket. He stands to gain a hundred and fifty thousand when this deal goes through, and he isn't going to mess that up for a measly, twenty-five grand. If he calls again, tell him things are fine, and I'll get in touch with him when I get back Sunday night."

"Sunday night? You're not due home for another week."

"I know, but there has been a slight change of plans. I'll be on the 7:20 flight Sunday night. Can you take the Hornet and pick us up?"

"Sure. By the way, how are you and Bobby doing?"

"The little fellow and I are coming along pretty well. I think we've come to a new understanding. I'll tell you all about it on Sunday. How are things going with you and that pretty 'Ivory Tower'?"

"Fine. We had a beautiful weekend in Salinas's right after you left. We're getting together Friday night. I thought we might space around some and then go to a movie, or dinner."

"Sounds great. Bobby and I are going to try and catch a glimpse of Kohoutek tonight from the hotel roof. Today's January 15, and It's supposed to make its closest pass to the earth. At any rate, you take care of yourself, you ugly Portagee', and give my love to that woman of yours."

"I will."

"Bye. Oh, one more thing, Manny, Don't worry. Old Mury will take care of everything. And, I think you're doing a great job."

"Thanks. Bye."

TWENTY-TWO

Manny spent most of that weekend with the lovely, Michelle. Together they made love, danced and sang, and made love some more. Occasionally, Iris would surface to tell Manny that Rocket was ripping off him and Mury, and that there was something very wrong with the deal. She was more charitable towards Bobby, but felt that he too, was only interested in the 'pot' at the end of Mury's rainbow. Manny pushed aside her warnings and innuendoes. He wanted to have faith in both Mury and the deal.

Saturday, the couple bought a bottle of champagne, and Sunday they popped the cork when they picked up Mury and Bobby at the airport. As soon as the luggage was in the trunk of the company car, Iris lit a joint and the champagne flowed as the four drove back to Sourdough Sam's. Despite the bubbles and laughter, Manny could sense tension in the car. He figured all was not paradise in the relationship between the two men. He was right.

When they arrived at Sam's Iris immediately left stating she had to rise early in the morning, and Bobby went directly to the bedroom and shut the door. The writer and the manager sat down, and Mury told Manny about Bobby and the trip. The first half had been wonderful, and the last half, a disaster. The romantic train ride from Chicago to Boston had ended in failure. Bobby was more interested in having Mury as a friend and father figure which he never had, then as a lover.

Next, it was Manny's turn to fill Mury in on all the events that had transpired during his absence. Briefly, he reiterated the phone conversation with Rocket, the business matters relating to Sourdough Sam's and his relationship with Iris-Michelle.

There was one incident that Manny was eager to share with Mury, and that was the visit he took with Iris' friend, Gail, to see Betty Bathard

152

at the Inner Light Foundation. Betty was a psychic who had her own radio program, did public 'life readings', and lectured extensively on parapsychology. The particular lecture Manny had gone to hear was being held in a hall with high pyramid-shaped roof, and as soon as he walked through the door he could feel his psychic energy begin to soar.

As he and Gail waited in line to be received by Betty, Manny felt more psychically inclined than ever before. Turning to a man behind him, Manny told him that he felt the man was suffering from a bad back. The man was shocked at Manny's intuition, as that was the exact reason he had come to see Ms. Bathard. Manny proceeded to tell the man how he had injured his back and suggested various remedies to relieve his pain.

Gail and Manny were greeted by Betty. Gail, who had met the woman before, handled the introductions. Manny was immediately convinced he had met this woman before. He felt as if he had known her all his life. No words were exchanged, and the two simply touched hands. Sparks of communication flew between their eyes. As Manny and Gail made their way to their seats, Betty stepped up on the stage.

A portion of Betty's lecture was devoted to demonstrating exercises to increase psychic energy in the individual or collective group. One exercise involved a few moments of meditation by members of the audience, who were instructed to shake their hands good and hard after they were finished. The psychic then instructed everyone to hold their hands in the air, palms toward the stage. Betty then held her hands up, and pointed her fingers toward the audience, and slowly began to wave them up and down. The results were amazing to Manny. He could actually feel Betty's energy moving up and down on his own palms with each wave of her hands. Next, Betty began her 'reading'.

Closing her eyes, she began meditating. After a few moments, her eyes opened and she spoke into the microphone.

"I have been in touch with my guides who tell me that we are living through a period of time when many people who once lived in Atlantis are now residing in San Francisco." Manny felt as if she were speaking directly to him.

"These people have been sent here to reaffirm their belief in the ONENESS of the universe and mankind. After a brief stay in San Francisco, these people will spread throughout the country preaching the words of the LAW OF ONE to all who will listen," the rich melodious voice rang out over the hall, causing Manny to feel as if he were floating three feet off his chair.

Mury was convinced the Betty Bathard lecture, and Manny's reaction to it, was one more sign that their cocaine deal was a righteous endeavor. The conversation moved from the mysteries of the universe, to the realities of the cocaine deal.

Mury relayed the story of his sale of the sample of cocaine at the top of the Marriott Hotel. He said, although he had been scared to death, the deal had been relatively simple. He and Lenny had met the prospective buyers for dinner and drinks at the hotel restaurant. It was agreed that the half ounce of cocaine would go for nine hundred dollars. Envelopes were exchanged across the table, and the group got up to leave. The only snag occurred as they were on their way out of the restaurant. One of the buyers motioned to Mury into the vacant coatroom by saying he wanted to show him something. Mury not thinking anything odd about the request, was just about to follow, when Lenny grabbed him by the arm and ushered him out the door. Mury couldn't figure out what the hell Lenny was so upset about, but figured it was just his method of doing business.

"What about this deal for the ten percent you mentioned on the phone?" Manny was eager to hear the entire story, and Mury could get bogged down in details.

"Oh, that. Well, the next day we met the same two men again. They picked us up in this big black Cadillac, and we rode around while I explained the deal. They said they had to think about it, and we agreed to meet the next day."

"But you didn't?"

"No, we did. Unfortunately they couldn't raise the money. But at least I have the nine hundred they gave me."

"That's great, but where are we going to get another nine thousand?"

"Don't worry about it Manny. I'm the manager. If worse comes to worse, I can always borrow it from my brother, or we could buy less. Listen you crazy Porchagoose', I've been hassling with this for days now and I'm wiped out. I'm going to turn in. I'll see you in the morning."

"Okay, you big pig. I'll see you then. Oh, don't forget to give Bobby a kiss for me."

"I'm not sure that's such a good idea. The little fucker isn't talking to me."

As Mury got up to leave, footsteps could be heard in the next apartment. The two men listened silently until Manny broke in, "Sourdough Sam must be pacing again. He's been driving me crazy with it since he came back."

"He does that when he's scared," was Mury's reply.

*   *   *

The next morning Manny was the first one up. He headed down to the Deli to find a cup of coffee. Jerry and Margo, who were the first to arrive, usually had a fresh pot all made. Instead, Manny found the pot empty and the warehouse deserted. As he quickly heated the water, he nearly tripped over a stack of breadmaking kits.

The kits that had been packaged during the Christmas rush were now being shipped back in droves to Sourdough Sam's. P&H Distributors hadn't been able to sell many, and unfortunately, Lenny's little deal had one overlooked clause. Any kits that weren't sold were to be returned to Sam's and didn't have to be paid for. Consequently, the entire warehouse was now stacked, floor to ceiling, with unsold kits. Wandering through the maze of stacks, Manny thought of Lenny's other bad decisions. He made his way back to the Deli just in time to see Jerry and Margo through the window. They were crossing Clement Street and heading for their Hudson. Manny ran to the door and called hello, but they merely glanced his way and jumped in the car.

Hearing footsteps, Manny turned and saw a bleary-eyed Bobby just pouring a cup of freshly brewed coffee. Manny told him about the couple's strange behavior, but Bobby didn't seem to think it was all that odd.

"They probably didn't see you."

I know they saw me, Manny thought to himself, but tried to shrug off the uneasy feeling.

Just as Manny was adding sugar to his second cup of coffee, Sourdough Sam, himself, brushed by without a word and headed straight for the office.

"What's he doing here?" Manny whispered to Bobby. "He's hardly ever down here, and never in the morning."

At that instant, Jack Sterns, the treasurer, appeared, and behind him, Mury. Sourdough Sam re-emerged from the office and the three men poured coffee. Mury told Manny and Bobby to stay up front while the three men talked a few things over. Manny watched as they disappeared into the back of the building. He and Bobby had finished their third cup of coffee, but the powwow between the three men still hadn't broken up.

Manny and Bobby decided to walk to the beach. It was a beautiful day, and the sun felt good on Manny's face. They watched the waves and sat in the sand discussing Bobby's feelings about Mury. He explained to Manny why he definitely wanted to leave Mury. By the time they arrived back at the warehouse, an hour had passed.

Jerry and Margo had returned, but their greeting was less than enthusiastic. Ned had arrived, and his expression as he sat at Mury's desk was blank. With the same expressionless face, he informed Bobby and Manny that he had orders not to allow them back in the warehouse or factory. When asked why, he responded with a shrug of his shoulders.

Manny asked the next question. "Where's Mury?"

"He went upstairs."

Bobby and Manny headed for the back passageway, but had only taken a few steps, when Ned told them the passage had been blocked off.

"You have to go outside and use the other door if you want to get upstairs."

As usual they found Mury's door unlocked, and Manny spoke first. "What did they say, Mury?"

"I'm fired."

TWENTY-THREE

As it turned out both Mury and Bobby were fired. And since Manny was paid out of Mury's pocket, in essence he was fired, too. Sourdough Sam and the company treasurer were concerned about the checks totaling fifteen thousand dollars that had been written on the Sourdough account to purchase jewelry. They hinted they might press charges for both forgery and embezzlement. Neither Mury nor Manny could find out how much, if anything was known about the cocaine deal. No one in the plant was talking, not even the loyal Ned. The only clue they had, was that people were afraid the place was bugged, and no one wanted to be implicated. It was easier for Manny to understand people's fear and their reluctance to get involved than it was to understand the cold treatment they gave Mury. At one time or another he had helped each one of the staff, and it hurt him to have them turn their backs on him. This in turn, hurt Manny.

Although Sam and Jack Sterns both stressed they felt Mury was an honest employee with strong loyalty to the company, it still didn't ease the rejection. Even the term employee smacked of insult. Mury, as manager, had sacrificed much of his personal life to help the company grow from a nickel and dime mail order operation, to a thriving business concern on the brink of financial acclaim.

Manny was particularly hurt by the company's attitude about Mury, and their hints at police charges. As far as he was concerned, Mury had done nothing illegal. The money from the cocaine deal was not to be used for Mury personally, but only to finance several operations that would benefit Sourdough Sam's. Manny felt he should be treated as a hero, not a petty crook.

Manny's main concern at this time was how much was known about the dope deal. He finally managed to get Margo, the one person he trusted, alone. She told him that she and Jerry had an idea that there was a lot more going on with Rocket than just a jewelry transaction. She had no idea, however, if Sam or anyone else knew about the cocaine. That left Manny trying to decide what to do about his connection back east.

His instincts told him to do nothing. The deal hadn't progressed far enough for there to be any serious threat to Al and his anonymous friends. Manny felt secure in that area.

The next problem was survival. Mury had been given three days to vacate his apartment, and the question was where to go from there. Manny knew that temporarily, he could stay with Iris along with Mury and Bobby. But that still didn't solve the problem of how they would live financially. Mury was out of a job and with him, Manny. The ex-manager and writer sat down together to smoke a bowl and to try and make some decisions and also to figure out what had gone wrong.

Manny was convinced the informer had been Jerry Wilson. He'd never trusted the man with his shifty 'cat eyes' and arrogant manner. The second most likely candidate was Randy. Manny remembered the day he had placed the frantic phone call to Mury in Boston. Later that night Randy had stopped by for a friendly drink. That is itself was odd, as the two men never socialized and could hardly be considered friends. Randy had proceeded to question Manny about Mury's trip. Manny had given the standard cover story about negotiations with Pillsbury and Bundt Pans, which was partly true. Randy seemed to buy the story, but his behavior towards Manny that night was very odd. At one point, he had picked up one of the toy soldiers from Manny's prized collection and cut off the legs. Randy tried to laugh it off as a hilarious joke, but Manny didn't think it was very funny. There had been a definite air of hostility about the act. At the time, Manny had attributed it to Randy's somehow, having found out about the evening he'd spent with his girlfriend, Jennie.

On the other hand, Sourdough Sam could have been behind the visit. He and Randy were very close, and maybe he had suggested Randy snoop around. Round and round Mury and Manny went trying to pinpoint who and why. Finally they gave up and decided to go out for drinks and a bit to eat. As Manny went to shower, Mury went to dig up some boxes to be used in packing.

In the shower, Manny could feel his body begin to react to the dope. He was becoming so sensitized that he could feel each separate molecule of H2O as the water streamed over him. Soon his mind began to have a similar reaction. Thoughts began to reel by in rapid succession. What if Margo and Jerry and Ned are right and the apartment is bugged? Could that be? Manny's imagination began to run wild, and he tried to calm himself down.

Hell no, he thought. That's only in the movies. This is real life. Still, what if the narks do know about the whole deal. We could be put in jail. Of course I could write in jail. As Manny lathered soap over his body, he visualized himself in a comfortable cell hammering out his novel at a typewriter. As he rinsed the suds off, a new and unpleasant thought struck him.

What about Al's possible connections with the Mafia? What if they think we double crossed them? What if they think we led the police to them? They might try and rub us out before we could explain!

Manny was paranoid now, and scared. He turned off the water and jumped out of the shower. He threw a towel around himself and walked into the bedroom where Mury was packing.

He whispered in his ear. "This place might really be bugged. Maybe we ought to think about getting out of here sooner than we planned." He tried to sound calm but he could feel waves of fear streaming from his body, and Mury picked up on it.

His voice, when he answered Manny, was barely audible. "Maybe we should go see Dr. Hank. He's the only lawyer I know, and I think he likes me well enough to help us."

"Okay," Manny whispered, "why don't you throw a few things in our brief cases while I shave? Keep talking like we're only going out to dinner. Once we're out of here we can make our escape."

"Good," Mury replied, "Hurry with your shaving. I'll get everything ready. They told me I could use the car until I was settled, but that might be bugged, too. We'll make them think we're going to use it, but instead we'll take a bus. They might trace a cab."

Manny finished his shave, and Mury quickly threw things in the briefcases. At the same time, they kept a running conversation going about dinner and how they'd take the car. They even managed to crack a few jokes to convince the narks' of their plans. Manny was just leaving the bathroom, when Mury brushed by him carrying a small plastic a bag. Manny was already out in the hall before it registered with him what Mury had in mind. He rushed back into the bathroom just in time to watch Mury flushing down the toilet, the last quarter once of cocaine. Manny wanted to scream, although he understood how Mury felt. The only words he managed to utter were, "Let's hurry."

A few minutes later they were walking up Thirtieth Street. For their disguise, the two men wore suits and dark glasses and carried briefcases. Catching the Geary Bus, they headed downtown, but had only ridden a few blocks when they noticed dark man in a business suit eyeing them suspiciously. They quickly rose and got off at the next stop. When they were sure they weren't being followed, they hopped another bus which deposited them at the Greyhound Terminal. They had decided they world call Dr. Hank from the terminal and then catch a cab to the Trailways station. Anyone trying to follow them would, hopefully, be thrown off the track.

Mury placed a call to Dr. Hank, who told them to come right up and see him at his ranch. Then Manny placed a call to Iris. He assured her they were fine and would see her in a few days. He also told her the dope deal was breaking up. As he hung up the phone, Mury who had been standing behind, gave him a nasty look.

"Who did you call?" His voice was angry and full of suspicion.

Manny felt crushed. Mury didn't trust him, not even after all they had been through together.

"Iris." As he spoke a tear rolled down his face.

As the two men waited for a cab, Mury apologized. Manny was hurt but he understood where Mury was coming from. His whole world was collapsing around him. The people he loved the most and had taken care of, had turned against him, and for all he knew, he could go to jail, or even be killed. As they stood on the curb looking at each other, Mury Said, "Who is God?"

"I am," answered Manny

"Me too," Mury replied.

The two brothers shook hands.

TWENTY-FOUR

As they rode the Trailways bus to Dr. Hank's ranch in Eureka, the two men began to calm down. Manny taught Mury a card game called honeymoon whist, and as the bus moved away from the city, the two men began to joke about their hasty flight from the apartment. The ride seemed quick, and soon they were pulling into the Trailways terminal in Eureka.

The exhausted fugitives were met by a young man wearing spectacles who introduced himself as Dr. Heinrich Von Stuben's son. He ushered them into a VW bus for the twenty mile ride to the ranch. Manny dozed in the back seat as Mury protected the young man's mind for his feelings about existence.

At the ranch, the astute Dr. Hank, immediately sensing the two men's physical and emotional exhaustion, insisted on putting off any legal talk until the following morning. Acting more like a concerned and compassionate human being than a lawyer, he offered them food and drink. Soon the two weary men were shown to the guest room and as was the custom, everyone at the ranch retired early. Manny felt good that Dr. Hank treated them more like guests that alleged criminals. Exhausted, he quickly fell asleep. Beside him, Mury was already snoring.

The next morning, although the sky was overcast and hazy, it didn't detract from the feeling of peace and beauty which permeated the entire ranch. After breakfast, Manny and Mury met with Dr. Hank to discuss the legal implications of their potential case. Manny was particularly anxious to learn if he could be involved as a conspirator.

Mury did most of the talking; explaining to the lawyer how he felt the cocaine deal had been originated for the benefit of Sourdough Sam's. Dr. Hank was very understanding, but told Mury he felt he had fallen into the trap of believing too much of his own bullshit.

Mury was too shaken to reply and merely nodded his head in agreement. In reality, both Mury and Manny felt what they had done was right. It had been their decision to go through with the deal, and they had no regrets. Now they were prepared to face the consequences.

Dr. Hank said it might not be necessary for them to face any consequences. He was particularly interested in Sourdough Sam's treasurer. He couldn't understand why the man had authorized Rocket's large checks, especially since in each instance; the bank manager had called him for personal approval. Dr. Hank didn't think he had acted in the best interest of Sourdough Sam's, and felt this might be a point in Mury's favor. Once again, he made Mury go over every detail of the deal. When he was finished with Mury, he had Manny elate his version. Finally, he told them his fee would be five thousand dollars. Mury said he felt he could raise that amount. The meeting ended with Dr. Hank promising to investigate each aspect of the case thoroughly, and advising the two fugitives to stay away from Sourdough Sam's.

TWENTY-FIVE

"I don't care what you say; I'm not lifting a finger to help unless you take the laundry out of it!" Manny complained.

"Look, Manny, it's much simpler is we just move it with everything still inside. That was we don't have to make two trips."

The two men had reached a stalemate. Mury couldn't understand why Manny wouldn't help him carry the large cedar wood dresser down the steep staircase with the drawers still full of clothes and the wardrobe stuffed with a large duffle bag full of dirty laundry.

"If that's the way you want to move it. Go ahead. But you move it alone." Manny was adamant.

Up until this point, moving day had gone smoothly. Following their return from Dr. Hank's Eureka retreat, the two men had followed his advice and made plans to vacate the Sourdough Sam's premises. Ned and Jerry had been secured to help with some of the things, and Mury had made plans to store his belongings at his parents' home near Sacramento. Manny was going to move the few things he had to Iris's apartment. She had agreed to let him move in with her.

"All right, have it your way." Mury removed the drawers and laundry and soon the dresser, along with Manny's few boxes of clothes, chess table, and waterbed were safely packed in another faithful Ryder Rental.

At Iris', the two men met their second challenge of the day. The problem was how to move Manny's waterbed up three flights of stairs, over banisters, and around the lolly columns that supported the exposed staircase. The king-sized frame had been built by Manny while he and Susan were still living together. He had upholstered it in brown leatherette, and it was one of his prized possessions.

Finally, after much cursing and sweating, the bed was installed in Iris's bedroom. An exhausted Manny vowed never to move the bed again.

Relaxing over glasses of chilled wine, the trio of Ivory Tower, Sagittarius, and Pisces commented on how well they worked together. Since Mury and Manny were in essence unemployed and since Iris was dissatisfied working for her 'repping company', the group decided to continue their working relationship and form their own 'repping' company. It was agreed that the next weekend when a large gift show came into town, Manny and Mury would secure passes from Iris who had to be there anyway to man the booth for Burns and Manville.

That night, Mury slept on the bearskin rug in Iris' living room, and the next morning the trio trucked up to Sacramento in the Ryder sipping 'trucking wine' and singing all the way. While the two men transported Mury's excess belongings to a storage locker, Iris remained at Mury's house to become acquainted with his Libran mother.

Leaving Mury at his parent's home, Iris and Manny drove back to Daly City in high spirits. They finished the last of the wine and shared a joint. After returning the Rental, the tired but happy lovers headed up the stairs to the apartment. Half way up it began to dawn on the pair that they were not a 'living-together-couple'. The camaraderie and pleasant glow from the day began to fade as the reality of their decision took hold.

"Where the hell am I going to store your stuff, Silva? My apartment is already crowded," Iris half mumbled and she re-arranged her belongings to make room for Manny's things.

"Don't worry. We'll find room." Manny wasn't the least bit concerned. His first priority was to fill his beloved waterbed.

While Manny hooked up a hose and began filling the plastic mattress, Iris noisily jammed his clothes into her already overcrowded closet. Clearing an infitesimal space in the linen closet for his shaving kit and contact lens case, Iris continued her grumbling. She was still complaining about the lack of space when she shoved his chess set and table into the only empty corner of the living room. Iris had lived alone most of the thirty-three years, and the disruption of her possessions from their long standing places did nothing for her sense of security of her disposition. Exhausted, the couple smoked a joint and retired to the freshly filled waterbed. Promptly, they had their first fight over whose turn it was to fill the water glass.

A night's sleep did nothing to ease the transition from lovers to live-ins. The next morning Manny woke to the sounds of Iris cursing as she prepared for work and complained about the mess Manny's shaving things and lens kit was making in her linen closet. Manny's kiss, as he rose to send his love off to work, was returned by a brisk command to use the jar of coins by the telephone to do the laundry. Being the eldest of ten children, Manny was used to sharing household chores and washing clothes; but something in Iris's tone brought out the mule in him, and as the day passed he conveniently forgot to do the laundry. Fight number two.

As the first week together ended, minor skirmished, over who filled the water glass and who washed the clothes, escalated into larger battles over whose work was more important, and whose work was really 'work' at all. Iris was unhappy because Manny was home writing rather than holding down a regular job. Even though his unemployment checks had started rolling in and he was sharing half of the expenses, Iris still resented the fact that she had to go out to work while he only 'sat at home writing.' She didn't want to be involved with a man who was a nobody; and unemployed would-be writer. Only a famous author would do for the Ivory Tower. Of course, she wasn't willing to wait while he completed his first book to see if there was a chance he might become famous and rich. She wanted instant overnight success or nothing. She couldn't understand why he couldn't work at a regular job during the day and write at night. Manny tried to explain that writing was work; that his book was his job. However, with no pages coming out of his typewriter the last few weeks, it was difficult to show Iris his serious intentions.

Then there was the running battle over Susan, Manny's wife. Iris was still putting pressure on Manny to divorce Susan. He couldn't understand why his relationship with Susan bothered Iris so much, while the letters and phone calls he received from Miranda Walsh, who by now had moved to Chicago with her husband and children, had no effect. He felt that much of Iris' dissatisfaction as well as her bad moods stemmed from her problems at work.

Trying to be the best gift saleswoman in the world was hard on Iris. She felt she should advance more quickly within the company, but all Burns and Manville would hand her were the

Mama and papa' trade, small retail stores. She resented that the two men who owned the company gave themselves the big department store trade. These required little let work and afforded high commissions. Her resentment built during the day and at night she took it out on Manny. Michelle began making fewer appearances and Iris' muscles turned back into piano wire. Despite all the battles and the running threat of competition between them over who was the best and who was going to be more successful, Manny still loved Iris deeply. He felt that if she would only get used to sharing her life with another human being, their relationship could work.

One night, after a particularly vicious battle, things came to a head, and the two sat down to talk it over. Iris told Manny she felt he didn't understand how hard she worked. She felt that if he could only see her at work one say, he would have more empathy for her problems. It was decided that the next day he would accompany her to the gift show. Besides, Manny could start looking for lines that their own company might like to represent.

Iris had given Manny an entrance badge from Burns and Manville, and he spent a good part of the day searching the rows of booths for gift items to sell. He enjoyed the atmosphere of the big showplace, and the atmosphere of the cocktail lounge even better. It was good to be out of the house, and he was well received by Iris's salesmen friends. The couple began feeling better about each other. When they got home that night, Michelle filled the water glass and after a romantic dinner, the two went to bed. They were lovers once again.

TWENTY-SIX

"Kkkkkrrrryyyyaaaannnnaaaannnnda . . . . ." was the Gregorian chant as Iris' little blue bug chugged its way up the hills in route to Nevada City, California.

Kyrananda, founder and spiritual leader of the yoga community known as Ananda Community Village, was the disciple of Yogananda who wrote, "Confessions of a Yogi." The Community, founded in 1968, had been in existence for six years making it one of the most successful communes to spring from the social revolution of the sixties. Economically self supporting, Ananda Village produced carob candy, incense, and body oils along with a bean sprouting kit. It was the sprouting kit which drew the newly formed business trio of Mury, Manny and Iris to Nevada City. They had discovered the group at the gift show and felt their kit might be a possible line for them to represent.

Mury had been particularly drawn to the bean sprouting idea as it reminded him of Sourdough Sam bread making kits. Manny, less enthusiastic about the product, was prompted to make the trek after talking with the group's financial leader, Joytish, an elfish looking yogi who resembled George Harrison and had a personality combining pure spirituality with a wonderful sense of humor. Joytish had invited the trio to visit Ananda Village to discuss a possible business alliance. The only member of the trio, who wasn't thrilled about the Mung Bean People, as Mury had christened the group, was Iris.

Iris had preferred a company named EROTICA that dealt exclusively with oils and sexy perfumes. She had experience with selling love oils in the past and felt it was a much more attractive item to represent then mung beans. She had found the booth at the gift show and had been invited to visit the company's showroom by the president, Dan, a Rocket lookalike, who in the forty-fifth year of his life had divorced his wife, sold his plumbing company, and gone into the love oil business. One visit to the attractive showroom located in the expensive Mill Valley Mall made EROTICA her first choice.

It was only majority rule, and the constant pressure of Mury and Manny that made her agree to visit the Mung Bean people now, and EROTICA, later. Still, Iris was not thrilled about the visit, and as the group approached Nevada City there was tension in the small car.

The only thing the trio did agree on as they drove was their plan not to visit EAST AFRICIAN IMPORTS. Manny had found their booth at the gift show and while the three admired the lovely ivory statues and colorful paintings, each felt the art work would be difficult to market. As Iris and Mury argued the pros and cons of marketing mung bean sprouting kits, Manny worried about how to keep the two from each other's throats.

Iris and Mury had been arguing since the previous night. The major conflict was rivalry. Both Iris and Mury had been in business before, and each considered themselves the more experienced and knowledgeable salesperson. Iris had worked independently, and Mury had been a company manager. Consequently, neither would admit they might possibly be equals in an equal partnership.

Gone was the camaraderie of the moving experience. More and more Manny found himself in the middle of their petty power struggles and at times he would scream at both friends out of sheer frustration. The problem was he loved them both and wanted them to get along. He began to realize that coupled with their games of one upsmanship was a mutual distrust. Mury, although he admitted to respecting parts of Iris' character, still felt resentment at her treatment of Manny. He felt at bottom line she was a ball-buster. Iris, on the other hand, although admitting that Mury was an intelligent person with much potential, felt he had trouble getting his 'shit' together and cited the dope deal as an example. In her eyes, Mury was responsible for not foreseeing the potential problems.

With the beauty of the Sierras surrounding them, and the chant of Kyrananda resounding in the car, the tension between the two began to ease. Up to that point, the trip had been hell. Iris had threatened to turn the car around if Mury didn't treat her with more respect. At one service station where she stopped for gas, Iris had let her hostility out on the station attendant.

The gas crisis had finally hit the west coast, and Iris had developed an intense dislike for all attendants. They appeared to her as grease stained men who overnight had become kings dispensing a precious liquid to the common horde.

Manny watched in horror as Iris, angry because the man who was servicing a line of twenty cars at the pumps wouldn't take the time to wash her windshield, jumped out of the car and began washing the window herself. As she finished the job, she threw the bucket on the ground and flung the rag at the man. Although Mann loved her dearly, he had to admit that sometimes she could be a ball buster, and much of her anger was difficult to understand.

They were nearing Ananda community Village, and Manny wanting to present a united front, tried to use reason to calm Mury and Iris. He mentioned that as business partners, they needed to make a good first impression on the Mung Bean People. He urged them to cool their personal tensions and present a calm professional business manner. As the car turned into the drive leading to the village center, the two adversaries put on their bust business smiles.

Surprisingly, the Yogis had a very together financial organization and were good businessmen. In addition to paying fifteen hundred dollars to join, a new member had to provide for his own living space and work twenty hours a week for the commune. Although Manny was impressed by their business expertise and admired some of the spiritual teachings, he felt it would be difficult for him to ever become a member of such a group, as a prerequisite was pledging an oath of devotion to Kyrananda, the spiritual leader.

Joytish, the elfish financial leader, apparently had no such qualms. He led the trio on a tour and pointed out the home he himself had built in the mountains. It was beautiful. The structure had been built in the shape of a geodesic dome. The dome was twenty feet high and had Plexiglas sheets inserted on three sides of the pentagon-shaped building. The end affect was three picture windows affording a breathtaking view of the valley below. A fourth Plexiglas panel was inserted in place of part of the roof over the loft section of the home. A viewer, lying on his back, was treated to a clear exposure of the northern California sky.

Manny was impressed by the home, especially its shape. He had come to believe that the natural energy of life force that creates the living world was increased as it passed through geometric shapes like a triangle or pentagon. Living in a geodesic dome had to be a high energy experience. Joytish explained that building a structure out of those shapes was very complex.

That night the trio shared a vegetarian meal with Joytish who acted as chef. It was excellent. After dinner the partners made suggestions for boosting production by improving the design of the sprouting kits. Joytish gave his approval by asking the group to handle the community's mung bean business.

Later that night, Manny and Mury bandied spiritual philosophy while Joytish add his own views. Manny felt the man was an open and responsive human being. Joytish explained that most people told him he was all right for a "freaked out yogi." It wasn't long before it was time for bed, and the four climbed the stairs to the loft.

Before taking out his contact lenses, Manny took one more glimpse of the bright stars overhead and settled down to sleep. Soon he felt the soft warmth of Michelle's hand sliding across his abdomen and into his underwear. They made love, soft and quiet under the moon between the freaked out yogi and the star-crazed Sagittarian.

TWENTY-SEVEN

"Why the hell can't I get anything done on this damn book? What the hell is wrong with me today, anyway?"

Manny continued pacing around the living room. He went to the door of the kitchen and started to say something to Iris. She was immersed in paper work for Burns and Manville. He decided not to interrupt her and continues his journey around the room.

"Maybe it was the scene at EROTIA the other day. We were so sure they wanted us to represent them. After the deal worked out so well with Joytish, he had our hopes so high. And that Dan. Sure, ETOTICA has a good set up, but he lets those kids run the place while he takes off to play. He's letting himself lose control of his own business."

Manny stopped and looked out the window.

"The biggest blow was their doubting our credibility as reps. Sure we're a new company, but so are they. Fuck. I'm feeling worse, now. What the hell is the matter with me? Gas crisis . . . gas crisis. I've got to stop thinking about the gas crisis. I saw the edge of it the other day when I was having Iris's car filled up."

Manny sat down at the table, and a strange feeling came over him. He couldn't put his finger on it, but it made him uneasy.

'The poem, remember the poem. Shut up, I'm getting to it. I've got to get some work done, even if it's just for my own ego. Okay, come on. Write a poem about the gas crisis.'

His fingers started to type:

'Gas is at the bottom of the energy crisis.

It is also at the bottom of my stomach

And sometimes it can be a pain in the ass."

He stared at the words.

"Well not too bad, but it has to go around and reach the beginning again. People have to laugh at the crisis or they won't' get over it. I wonder if it's signaling the beginning of the cataclysms. I hope so, although I'd have to get back home before it happened. Al right, enough wondering. Start to write. Jesus, I feel so miserable; I just don't want to do this."

He attacked the keys once more:

"Oil is at the bottom of the gas crisis.

It is also at the bottom of my boat

Am it can be as slippery as hell."

"Hey, not too bad for a second verse, abut where can I take it from here."

Manny circled the room once more and went back to the desk;

"Conglomerates are at the bottom of the oil crisis. They also clog up my toilet bowl and smell like shit."

"Jesus Christ." He screamed and tore the paper from the typewriter and threw it in the trash just as the telephone rang.

"Iris, Iris, can you get that? I'm right in the middle of something."

"All right, but next time it's your turn."

As Manny put a fresh piece of paper into the typewriter, he could make out Iris's end of the telephone conversation:

"Hello . . . . I'm fine, too . . . . . . Heard from Mury? No, Mrs. Nestor. Isn't he staying with you? . . . . How long has he been at the Y? . . . . We haven't heard from him . . . . You got a call from the police? When? . . . . Of course. We'll call around and see what we can find out . . . . No, Mrs. Nestor, we'll call you back as soon as we find something out."

As soon as he heard the word police, Manny went to the phone. Hanging up, Iris turned to him.

"Mury's mother got a call from the San Francisco police. They told her Mury had been arraigned, but she didn't know where he'd been taken. She asked us to try and find out more about it. Dr you think Sourdough Sam could be behind this?"

"I don't know, but I doubt it. I've been feeling something strange was happening."

"Look, I'll call the main station and see if I can find something out. Poor Mury." Michelle was back.

Michelle dialed the number, and Iris spoke using her business voice.

"Hello. This is Iris Ivory calling. I'm inquiring about a friend of mine, one Mury W. Nestor. Could you tell me if you have a record of his being arrested, and if so, on what charges? . . . . . Yes, I'll hold."

Iris and Manny waited in silence. All at once the line came alive.

"Yes, I'm still here . . . . . You don't! His mother called me a few minutes ago and said the police had called her to verify that she had a son named Mury. I'm sure she didn't make that up . . . . I see, I see. I'll try them, then."

Iris hung up and told Manny there was no record of Mury having been arrested anywhere in San Francisco. But that the police suggested she call the federal lockup. She called information and dialed the number.

"Hello. I'm a friend of Mury W. Nestor. I've heard that he's been taken into custody by you people. Could you give me some information on him? . . . . . Yes, I'll wait."

Turning to Manny she said, "They're checking the records."

Once again a voice came back on the line.

"Hello . . . yes, I see. Thank you very much."

Iris turned to Manny, her face ash white. "Mury was arrested last night on a narcotics charge. He was released this morning on personal recognizance."

For a brief moment Manny nearly lost control. A series of thoughts ran through his mind. He imagined everything was over, and that the narks' were after him, too. They had taken Mury, and now he was next. He couldn't stand still, but he couldn't sit down either. He didn't know what to do, so he paced.

"I knew something was wrong. I just knew it. What the hell are we going to do? They could come and get me next."

There was a knock at the door and both Iris and Manny froze. There was a second knock.

"Should I answer it?" Iris whispered.

Manny composed himself and tried to sound cheerful.

"I said I would go to jail if necessary. You better answer it."

Iris looked through the peephole. "I can see a blue uniform cap."

Manny gritted his teeth and opened the door.

"Hello. Is this the residence of Miss Iris Ivory?"

"Yes, it is."

"I have a package for her."

It was the mailman.

TWENTY-EIGHT

Three weeks had passed since Manny and Mury had been asked to vacate the Sourdough Sam establishment, and Iris and Manny wondered if the narks had only just now found out about the cocaine deal. If so, did that mean that Sam himself had turned Mury in, and if that was the case, was Manny to be arrested, also. No questions could be answered until they talked to Mury.

All day they tried to re ach Mury. First they called the San Francisco YMCA where Mury's mother told them he had been staying, and left a message. Next, they called Mrs. Nestor to see if Mury had been in touch. Finally, they called Bobby. No one had heard from Mury. But the man at the Y said he had gone out earlier that morning.

The day passed in a flurry of telephone calls, panic, and paranoia, and arguments between Iris and Manny. Tensions were high.

Finally, at seven that night, Iris got through to Mury at the Y. However, it was Michelle who did the talking.

"Mury, it's Iris. Your mother called and told us you were arrested. How are you holding up? . . . . Listen Luv, you can't stay at the Y. You need company right now. Why don't you stay with us until you can get your head together? . . . Good. Manny and I will be down to pick you up. Pack your clothes and be waiting . . . . . Yes, we thing you're pretty wonderful too. See you."

In twenty-five minutes Iris's blue Bug was parked in front of the Y, and Manny was at the front desk. The man gave him directions to Mury's room. One knock and the door was opened by a tired and haggard, but still smiling, Mury. The two men embraced like long lost friends. As Mury gave his friend a tour of his room, re relate the details of his arrest.

Two men had come to his room and asked if he was Mury Nestor. When Mury identified himself, they pulled out badges and told him he was under arrest for the sale of narcotics. They read his rights and asked where he kept the cocaine. Mury tried to tell them he didn't have any cocaine, but they tore his room apart anyway. Manny flashed on the earlier toilet-flushing-scene, and the incident seemed les paranoid than he remembered.

Manny asked Mury more about the sale and tried to find out if the narks were after him too.

"I just don't know. The warrant for my arrest was issued in Massachusetts, but the people who picked me up didn't seem to know anymore than that. Oh, I did find out something when I got to the station.'

"What?"

"Those guys I sold the cocaine to at the top of the Marriott on January 15 were narcotics agents. Jesus, I can't believe I drove around with those guys for two days explaining everything about the deal. Apparently they have the whole conversation on tape."

Big Al's warning flashed through Manny's mind. Don't go anywhere with people you don't know.

"Look Manny. I really don't think you are in any trouble. I kept my word and never mentioned your name, not even in the conversations with those two narks in Boston."

Manny breather a sign of relief and asked the big questions: "Who do you think turned you in? And how did the narks find out about the deal in the first place? They didn't mention Jerry Wilson did they?"

"No. Besides, I don't think it was Jerry." Mury's next statement shook Manny. "Only two people knew I was staying at the Y, Dr. Hank and Lenny."

"Lenny! How did he know?" Manny was exasperated.

"The night before I was arrested, I called him from here to see if anything could be salvaged from the dope deal. I told him if he thought of anything, to call me at the Y. It had to be Lenny."

Manny recalled the feeling of distrust about Lenny Solens. He had asked Mury not to bring him into the deal, but he didn't say anything about that now. Mury was probably feeling bad enough without being told, "I told you so."

As the two men made their way towards the elevator, Mury told Manny haw he was led handcuffed through the lobby and about his night in jail. Manny only hoped he wouldn't have to repeat the experience.

Outside the Y, Iris and Mury embraced warmly, friends once more. Soon the reunited trio were making their way back to Daly City.

The next morning Iris went to work as usual, leaving the two men drinking coffee laced with brandy as they discussed the failure of the cocaine deal. The morning passed quickly, and soon it was afternoon. Coffee gave way to pot and 'truckin wine' as the friends tried to figure out their next move. Bobby had been called and would be arriving the next day to help Mury find a new place to live. By the time Iris returned from work, the Pisces and the Sagittarius were high and mellow. After a long hard day at selling, Iris was not in a very good humor. The sight of the two cohorts laughing and drinking did nothing to improve her mood. She retired early leaving Manny and Mury still talking.

*   *   *

The 'Love unlimited' tape blasted in Manny's ears as Bobby's big Pontiac pulled away from the curb leaving a patch of rubber. This was the second day of their search for an earthly Nirvana for Mury, but like the day before, they could find nothing. By four o'clock they had visited a good fifty real estate agents and viewed so many apartments they had lost count. Tired and discouraged, they headed back to Daly City to collect Mury's things. He would be spending the night with Bobby.

Mury followed Manny up to the third floor landing. As many knocked for Iris to let him in, he noticed several familiar looking boxes outside the door. There was no answer, so Manny took out his key. It fit the lock as usual, but he couldn't get it to turn. He tried knocking again, but there was still no reply.

"I don't get it."

Meanwhile, Mury had found a note taped to the door frame. "I do. Read this."

Manny took the note and read it out loud.

"Manny—

"I could not take you and Mury any longer. You will find the rest of your things packed and stacked by the back door. Please don't try to get in touch with me as I have made up my mind and have nothing further to discuss with you.

Goodbye
Iris"

TWENTY-NINE

"SSSSaaaaaccccccrrrrraaaammmmmentooooo . . . . . .,"was the chant as Manny and Mury rode the Greyhound bus to Murray's parents, home. As they played hands of honeymoon whist, they kept up a running dialogue about none other than, Iris.

"She's a ball busting bitch," Mury began, his 'I told you so' attitude slipping through.

"I still love her," Manny countered. "It's just that sometimes she's hard to understand."

Manny was good and pissed at Iris, but her love for her made it hard for him to hate her. Still, even he had to admit to himself that one thing she had done disturbed him greatly. It had to do with his waterbed. All of his personal belongings had been packed neatly and nicely in boxes; even his sheets and pillow cases. The only thing she had made no provision for, was the return of his waterbed.

After he had read the note from Iris, Manny had run to the corner telephone booth and called Iris. Being her usual efficient self, she had hired an answering service to monitor her calls, so he couldn't get through to her directly. Manny left a message quickly and called her friend, Gail. When he mentioned the waterbed, Gail told him that Iris considered it hers now. Apparently she had taken his statement during the move about "never moving it again" as gospel. Infuriated, Manny was powerless to do anything about the bed.

One thing Gail said made Manny feel better. She told him that while the two of them were together, she had never seen Iris so happy. She told him how sorry she was, and how high her hopes had been for their relationship working. Still, like Mury before her, she couldn't resist adding that she, too, had warned Manny about Iris and men. She ended the conversation by saying:

"When she gets rid of a lover, she doesn't fool around."

As the bus paused to pick up some passengers, Manny felt a stab of pain. There was no way he could reach Iris now; she was of in her Ivory tower. The break had been complete, and Manny's heart was bleeding.

All many carried with him on the bus to Sacramento was one suitcase. The rest of his things were being stored at Bobby's. His mother offered to let Manny and Mury stay at her house, but the two friends felt a little rest in the quite suburbs of Sacramento was what they both needed at this point. They needed time to heal, and time to find a new direction.

Not everything was bleak. They still had their ace in the hole; the Mung Bean People. Since Iris didn't want anything to do with the two of them anyway, they world simply continue the business without her. An appointment had been made with Joytish while the trio had been up to Ananda for later that week, and Mury and Manny intended to keep it. Everything would be fine once the mung beans began to roll in. Mury's mother was a nervous wreck when she met them at the bus terminal. She didn't like driving in that part of the city.

"You never know if there're muggers lurking, or Lord knows what else." Her tension set the whole tone of their stay.

The Nestors lived in a beautiful ground level ranch house outside Sacramento. The development had been built on an almond orchard and the trees left standing wee in full bloom when Manny and Mury arrived, but Mury's eighteen your old sister, affectionately called Mossy by her brother, was on hand to greet them.

After breakfast the next morning, Mury put in a call to Joytish. He wanted to show his family that the two of them were still a business team to be taken seriously, and that the incident with Sourdough Sam was just that, an unfortunate incident. Neither of them were prepared for what they heard.

First Mury was told that their good and spiritual friend Joytish was too busy to come to the phone. Next, he was informed that Ms. Iris Ivory had already called the Mung Bean People to inform them that Mury and Manny had been involved in narcotics trafficking, as well as having ripped off an innocent company they worked for, for a great deal of money. In short, Mury was told point blank that all business deals were off.

"That ball busting bitch." Manny couldn't help himself from saying.

The phone call to the Yogis marked the beginning of the end in Sacramento. Instead of the restful nirvana they had envisioned, Mrs. Nestor's increasing nervousness infected everyone. Finally, the reason for her tension came out.

"I don't think it's right for an impressionable eighteen year old girl to be living in the same house with grown man who isn't even a relative. What must the neighbors be saying?"

They packed their bags and were soon playing cards on the bus en route to Alameda. The only place left to go was Bobby's.

Bobby's mother loved Mury. Not only had he always been gentle and sensitive towards her, but he had helped buy the house she lived in. Not only was she happy to have Manny and Mury she told them they could stay as long as they wanted. Unfortunately, her sentiments were not shared by the animal menagerie, two cats and two dogs, who shared the house, or Bobby.

Mury and Jimmy had been sharing the same bed; but that was all. Bobby had made it perfectly clear that he no longer wanted Mury as a lover, or a father-figure. Living in such close quarters, the already tenuous relationship was strained to the point of loud shouting matches and stony silences. Several nights as Manny lay on the living room couch fighting one of the dogs and cats for sleeping space, he could hear the two of them screaming at each other. Pretty soon they world have to move; life couldn't go on like this.

Things were easier during the day as both Bobby and his mother had jobs to go to. Bobby's job, however, was a sore point with Mury. It had come out that the man who had hired him as an insurance adjuster was also his new lover. Manny and Mury spent most of their days checking the newspaper ads for apartments. Bobby offered to take them into San Francisco the following Saturday to help them find a place to live.

Money was not the problem.. Manny had four hundred dollars left in his checking account and although he unemployment checks had ceased, he had recently applied for an extension which he felt sure he would get. Mury had most of the money left over from the cocaine transaction. Both men felt they could afford a nice apartment and were in agreement on what they wanted. The only stipulation Manny had was that it not be in a Gay section of town. Mury didn't protest and Saturday morning after Bobby drove them into town, they began their next search.

They walked into the fifth real estate office of the day feeling tired and discouraged. The apartments they had viewed were either too expensive, too small, or in unsuitable neighborhoods. Manny wondered if he would ever find a nice space to start work on his book once more.

The man behind the desk quietly listened to their needs and said, much to their surprise, he had just the place they were looking for. It was on Taylor Street, almost in North Beach, and it had two bedrooms, a kitchen and living room, and was partially furnished and had a heated swimming pool. Best of all, the rent was only $195.00 per month. Of course there were rumors that a murder had been committed in the apartment.

Soon, they were standing in front of a tall building staring at the sign that said; CRYSTAL TOWERS. The name caught the pair's imagination instantly. Not only was the apartment attractive and spacious, it had a balcony that overlooked the San Francisco bay and in particular, Alcatraz Island. The manager, who showed the apartment, actually seemed pleased to hear that Manny was a writer. She told them that Ayn Rand lived on the sixth floor, and Lauren Bacall had once lived there as well. Their minds were made up.

THIRTY

<hr/>

I Once I was a little snot
Someone picked me out
And was not.

Already, it is March. Manny and Mury have been living at CRYSTAL TOWERS for nearly a month, and nothing decent in the way of writing has come to Manny. He abandoned his novel about the cataclysms and decided to switch back to poetry. He had an idea for a book of poems that would tell a story rather than be an anthology. He wants the poems to tell people why they don't remember being on earth in other existences. Despite the idea, he has trouble writing.

Most of his days were spent sitting on the couch watching the boats in San Francisco bay pass by. Some days he walks to Ghirardelli Square and the Cannery. Often he walked out on the long cement pier opposite Ghirardelli. Occasionally he stopped to visit a friend of Iris's who worked at the Cannery. She manages, COMPLEX WEST, a gift shop. They talk, and she reads his poems. Always he feels lonely, and more and more he misses his children and Susan. Still, he swears to himself not to return to Massachusetts until he has completed a book; even if the book is not about the cataclysms.

Mury is now writing a book of his own. Most of his work is done at the library. When he returns to the TOWERS, he goes out on the balcony to meditate. He meditates with a worn baby blanket thrown over his head.

Lately, Mury has been meditating two, and even three times a day. He doesn't like to be disturbed, but once in a while Manny will interrupt him with a crazy poem like the one beginning this chapter. Manny likes to get a laugh out of him as there doesn't seem to be much to laugh at these days. Not even 'dirty dope' can be obtained to cheer up their days. As soon as their supplier heard about the drug bust, he refused to do business with them.

The brightest part of their week was going out to dinner. This they do two or three nights a week, like a ritual. The ritual involves dressing in their best business clothes and riding the cable car to a restaurant called GALLEY IN THE ALLEY. Then, they order a couple of drinks and chow down on the free appetizers; salami, cheese, chicken wings, and tiny meatballs. Sometimes, for a special treat, they hit the 99 cent movie on Stockton Street.

Sexually, things are very slow. Except for one quick night stand with Kate from COMPLEX WEST, Manny hasn't been laid since his last night with Iris. Mury isn't even doing that well. Something must be very wrong if neither of them can find a lover in all San Francisco.

Financially, they are holding their own. Manny's money went for security deposit and first month's rent, but Mury still has the money from the cocaine deal. They tried to engage in several business ventures, but so far none have panned out.

One of these ventures, THE WAY TO THE STARS, seemed especially promising and was discovered by accident. One day as Manny and Mury were on their way to the Hyatt Regency, they often went there to sit in the lobby sipping coffee and hoping some miracle would occur giving them the direction they needed, they found themselves standing in the front of the Trans American Pyramid Building.

Manny, in the middle of explaining his theory on the connection between geometric angles, energy, and pi, 3.14, had stopped to make a point. Mury said he remembered the Pythagorean theorem and had once read an article stating that the Trans American Building had been built facing north, south, east, and west, like the pyramid of Cheops. They started to walk around the base of the building, to see if they could pick up any vibrations, when all at once they felt a surge of energy. Thinking this might be an omen, they decided to look at the building register to see what type of businesses kept office space in the pyramid-shaped building. Moving down the ledger, their eyes both stopped on THE WAY TO THE STARS, 39TH Floor. The building didn't go any higher. They headed for the elevators.

The elevator stopped at the thirty-first floor, and a handsome black man carrying a movie projector entered. Mury exchanged pleasantries with the man who got off at the thirty-eight floor. When the doors opened on the next floor, both men had to stop themselves from gasping out loud. The room they entered was one to impressive splendor: plush, thick carpeting, dark wood panels, and three ornate desks each with a beautiful young secretary. It was the blonde who addressed them.

"Have you come in to answer our ad?"

The two men exchanged a look that implied, 'this is home.' Mury answered the woman. "I don't know about any ad, but whatever it is, we're definitely interested."

At that moment, the handsome, black man with the movie projector stepped through the elevator doors. One glance from the blonde and he introduced himself.

"I'm Vice- President of the company. Why don't you step into my office, and I'll explain how to find THE WAY TO THE STARS."

Manny and Mury learned that the company sold educational motivation. Similar to the power of positive thinking, the product came in a package of thirty-three taped lectures costing thirteen hundred dollars.

Stanton Themes, as the black man was called, ushered the two men into the next office and introduced them to the company president, Mr. Andrews. A self-made millionaire, he had used his educational motivation technique to sell real estate in Oxnard, California. Mr. Andrews seemed as impressed with Manny and Mury as they were with him, and it was agreed that the two of them start classes to become salesmen the next day at a well known San Francisco hotel.

As it turned out, not only were the classes boring, but some of the client-baiting techniques they were instructed to employ struck them both a distasteful. The tactics seemed contrary to so pure an idea as the power of positive thinking. Their enthusiasm for THE WAY TO THE STARS was sinking fast.

One day of selling and their enthusiasm left altogether. It was a rainy, miserable San Francisco day, and Manny was already soaked to the bone by the time he reached his first client. He had been instructed to contact a salesman and sell the plan to him. The man refused to see Manny. It was three o'clock and Manny had just seen his seventh client, with no better luck, when he decided to take a break and call home. Mury answered the phone and announced he had already retired. Manny hit one more client before making his way back to the pyramid building to return his kit. THE WAY TO THE START had turned out to be a way to the dumps.

The next venture proved no more promising in allowing them to find a direction, but at least it motivated Manny to start writing again. Mury had the idea to start a club for Atlanteans. Manny wrote a poem for the newspaper they planned to publish called, "Atlantis Rising," and they took out a phone under the name of Atlantis. That idea went the way of the stars, but at least they had the name in the phone book, and Manny had written a poem. The poem was one of his best in months, and it restored some of his self esteem. Maybe he could finish a book yet.

By now Mury was getting regular visits from a pre-trial patrol officer, so all new ventures were postponed until after the trial which had been scheduled for April 23rd.

THIRTY-ONE

The Catholic Church around the corner from the CRYSTAL TOWERES was big and old looking. Manny stood at the bottom of the steps watching the people file out from the previous Mass and trying to decide if he should enter. He had not come here to repent for any sins, or to find God. He was looking for inspiration. His book on life after death was still going badly, and he was frustrated. Despite several good ideas and a rough draft he wrote for the beginning section, he couldn't seem to find the right direction. Something was missing; some extra dimension he had to find. He walked up the steps and entered the heavy wooden doors of the church.

After Mass, the elderly priest stood on the steps to greet his parishioners. Manny walked by the man's smile and ignored his outstretched hand. No bolt of lightning had struck, and he had been as bored with the Mass as ever. No church could supply his inspiration; he would have to find it himself. In fact, the only thing the experience had done for him was to make him think of his children.

As he walked, tears began to roll down his cheeks. He missed his home and his three and four year old kids. He hadn't talked with Susan for some time now, and she wasn't even aware of Mury's arrest, or of his move to CRYSTAL TOWERES. It was time for a call to home.

"Hello Susan. It's Manny."

"Manny. I'm so glad you called. We've all been worried about you."

"How come?" Manny was surprised at the concern in the voice. It wasn't like Susan to show any emotional concern.

"I got a call from your friend Lenny, and he said you were in jail for stealing a lot of money from his company. I called the number you gave me at that woman Iris's house, but I kept getting an answering service. Where have you been?"

"I'm living in an apartment in San Francisco, but wait a minute, I don't understand. Lenny told you I was in jail?"

"Yes, and I told your father. He was very upset."

"Listen, I'm not in any trouble. Mury, the guy I told you about, the one who helped get me out here . . .?"

"Yes."

"He's in trouble, but I'm not involved . . . Well, not legally anyway. I've been upset about a lot of things that have been happening out here, but I haven't wanted to call you or the family and worry everyone. But, I assure you, I'm not in any trouble."

"Everyone will be glad to hear that."

"How are things at home? How are the kids?"

"Everyone is fine, the kids too. They miss you and enjoy the picture letters you send. Oh, I got the money back from our income tax."

"Great. Was it as much as we expected?"

"More. I never thought we'd get thirteen hundred dollars back with you only working five months last year, but I had a regular tax consultant do the forms, and that's what he came up with."

"Are we still going to split it down the middle like we agreed at Christmas?"

"Of course."

"All right then, this is what I'd like to do with my half. I'm missing the kids so much right now, I can hardly stand it, and well . . . what would you think about having them fly out here to visit? You could put them on the plane at Logan, and I'd meet them at this end. I'm sure the airline would take good care of them. It wouldn't be any different than hiring a babysitter for a few hours. Susan . . . ? What do you think?"

"I don't know. They're so young . . . No, I don't think I could take the chance."

"All right, then, why don't you come with them? I'll pay the fare. You'll love it out here. Maybe Mury will babysit a few nights so we can go out on the town. I'd love for you to see San Francisco; it's a fantastic city."

"It sounds wonderful, but I really can't afford to spend any extra money right now."

"You won't have to. I'll take care of everything. I've applied for an extension on my unemployment and it should come through by the time you arrive. I figure it will come to nearly eight hundred dollars so we'll have plenty of money. I miss all of you. You have to come."

"Well . . . I can't answer you right now. I have to think about it. I'll call the airlines and find out how much it would cost, and I'll decide then."

"That sounds fair. Susan, don't worry about that thing with Lenny. I'll write and explain everything to you. But believe me; I'm in no trouble whatsoever. Please tell the rest of the family that, too."

"I will. And. . . Thanks for calling. I'll write you after I talk to the airlines. We all miss you . . . bye."

". . . Bye. . . ." Hanging up the phone, Manny turned to Mury who had his head in the Sunday papers. Hey Mury, guess what?"

"What?"

"We're going to have visitors."

"Really, who?"

"Susan and the kids, who else?"

"Great, you fucker. I'm glad to see something has pulled you out of the dumps. Ever since Iris gave you the old axe, you've been pretty down. When are they coming?"

"I'm not sure, maybe next month. My unemployment should come through by then, and I'll have the money to show them San Francisco."

"Listen kid, seeing what a good mood you're in, why don't we go see our old friend Kyrananda?"

"Kyrananda?"

"Yep. I just read they're having some religious gathering over at the Masonic Temple. It's called a MEETING OF THE WAYS, and our friend Ram Dass, the one who wrote 'Be Here Now', will be there too. It might be worth the few dollars admission to hear what the old boy has to say."

"Why not. Krrryyyaaaaaannnnnaaannndaaaaa . . . !"

The MEETING OF THE WAYS was being held on two floors of the Masonic Temple. The auditorium, on the main flood, was housing the open forum led by several of the most well known religious leaders of the country. The basement was set up for a bazaar. Hundreds of small booths had been set up to display pamphlets and books on various religious doctrines, and an array of incense, beads, love oils, and potions.

Upstairs, Manny and Mury listened to their friends Kyrananda and Ram Dass, along with a famous Rabbi and other holy men, extol the youth of the day for their belief that that country could be changed for the better.

Downstairs, they ran into other friends, including Joytish who was running the Ananda booth. He seemed friendly enough, as he told them of his business dealings with Iris and verified that indeed, she had told him of Mury and Manny's shady reputation, but they could see the fear and distrust in his eyes.

Apparently, Iris was not actually handling the entire sprouting kit line. A man named John had taken over the line, and the kits were catching on. John had managed to introduce them into large department stores, and the profits were rising. As Joytish seemed visibly nervous, Manny and Mury said goodbye, wished him luck, and moved on.

Turing the corner, Manny ran into another old friend. Walt Ali. He was leading a community dance, and the two watched the dancers while listening to the drums and guitars.

Naturally, with Walt around, it wasn't long before they ran into Sabira. After having heard so much about Mury and his homosexuality, she was delighted to meet him in person. As they parted, Sabira asked if they would like to buy a hundred tabs of acid from her homosexual friend. They declined. Not only was there no money, there was no one they could sell it to.

The day passed quickly and pleasantly. Manny ran into several other old friends, but not Pat, the Theosophist he had met when visiting the Sufi Choir. He was mildly disappointed; it would have been nice to hold hands with her again.

THIRTY-TWO

"... What the fuck so you mean, my early out has been approved ...."

Manny had just typed the last lines of a poem about his experience in Vietnam. It had been emotionally draining to transport himself back five years to try and recapture his feelings at the time.

He wanted the poem to show people the wars effect on the individual soldier. As he read over what he had written, he was pleased. Technically, he considered it his best poem ever. He felt he had captured the transition the man made from the innocent young individual, who entered the war, to the soldier, and finally, to the crass, confused, and almost animal-like person who emerged at its end. He sat back and felt content. He knew exactly where this poem would fit in his book.

Anxious to repeat the success of the day before, Manny rose early on Tuesday and immediately went to his typewriter. He wanted to begin his poem on divorce, but unfortunately, something else came out instead. It was the Ivory Tower.

It had been two and a half months since Iris had bounced him out of her life, and in all that time he hadn't heard one word from her. The only news he had was from her friends, Gail and Kate. Gail told him Iris's car and apartment had been broken into, and that she suspected Manny as the culprit. Manny attributed her suspicions to her own guilt for having confiscated his waterbed.

Manny tried to dismiss all thoughts of Iris from his mind and concentrate on the divorce poem, but every time he started to write, words other than what he intended came out. It occurred to him that maybe he was love sick. He had heard of this strange illness and now he began to believe he might actually have it.

Certainly, he had never felt this way about any other woman. He loved and hated her at the same time. His mind re-ran thoughts of the things they had done together; loving things and painful things. In the short time the two of them had lived together, they had had more fights than Susan and Manny had in the entire five years they had been married. Still, fights and all, there was something about that woman.

He put his fingers to the keys once more and this time instead of fighting the thoughts, he allowed them to come.

WE TOUCHED AND KISSED AND HUGGED

We were so in love.
We cared if the world was looking.
I can still see us in that garden.
You said they were important Japanese plants.
I said they were pines, pruned to look like it.
It really didn't matter.
We watched the trickling little waterfalls.
Threw pebbles at the giant goldfish.
Listened to the birds sing tunes that only lovers hear.
We stood on the little wooden bridges and
We touched and kissed and hugged.

It was a poem about his affair with Iris and a time and place only she and Manny shared. He loved the poem and felt she would too. Even if she never wanted to see him again, she couldn't deny they had shared some beautiful moments together. He put the poem in an envelope and mailed it to her.

A few days later she called; she wanted to see him. She was still angry, but she wanted to see him and find out where they stood. Manny agreed, but used his waterbed as an excuse to cover his feelings. They made a date for the following Saturday.

As Manny hung up, part of him was elated, and part of him felt ill. He had missed Iris to the point of having actual physical pain, and yet, how would he break the news to Mury.

"You're a fucking asshole, Silva. She's nothing but a ball-busting bitch that hurt you and now you're going back for more."

"Look, I'm mad at her too, but I don't like you talking about her like that. I worked hard to build a relationship with her, and even if she may be the kind of woman who can only see a relationship from her own point of view, I have to see her again."

"Do what you want." Mury was hurt.

"I have to." Manny's mind was made up.

It was the first time since Kohoutek brought them together that the two friends had a disagreement they couldn't resolve. Manny could feel something break, and he was torn between his friendship with Mury and his love of Iris.

Saturday broke cloudy and cool, yet Manny could feel spring in the air. He took the cable car to Market and then BART out to Daly City. He wondered if Iris would be distant, and he wondered how she looked. He wasn't prepared for what he saw when she opened the door.

She looked awful. She had lost so much weight she looked emaciated. Her eyes wee dry and lifeless, and she resembled a walking corpse. Maybe their separation hadn't been any easier on her.

Walking in the sand-hills behind her apartment, they released their feelings. Iris screamed, Manny screamed. He wanted his waterbed; she said it belonged to her. They talked about their mutual anger and eventually their love. In an hour, they were spent and exhausted. Finally, they sat on a log and touched and kissed and hugged.

THIRTY-THREE

The day after Manny returned to the CRYSTAL TOWERS from his reunion with Iris, he half expected Mury to pick up their argument, but all his friend said was, "I'm glad to hear you and the Ivory Tower are hitting it off again."

Something about the way he said it made Manny feel he really wanted to say; "How can you be such an asshole to get yourself mixed up with that ball-busting bitch a second time?"

As it turned out, neither man mentioned it again. Mury was preoccupied with his impending trial, and Manny was immersed in his rekindling affair and his writing. His life revolved around his next meeting with Iris and his book.

At the moment, he was trying to figure out how to show a consciousness t raveling through space on its way to being born. He saw the idea in his mind but couldn't translate the thoughts into written words. He tried once more:

TIME
   AFTER
      TIME
        LIFE
     AFTER
   LIFE
     CARPENTER
       PRINCE
         MURDERED
           PRIEST
        PLUMBER
  SOME GOOD   SOME BAD

It wasn't quite right. He had to make the words seem as if they too, were moving through time and space.

He paused a moment, and his thoughts turned to Iris. God, he loved her. He wanted her almost as much as he wanted to be a successful author. They world see each other again on Saturday. Iris had suggested they drive to a secluded beach she had found along the coast. It crossed Manny's mind that she probably discovered the spot with some other guy, but he rationalized the pain quickly. If he wanted her, he would have to accept her for who she was.

He looked over what he had written and exclaimed, "Carrumba, I can't figure it out." He tore the paper out of the typewriter.

* * *

"Clang, clang, clang," went the cable car Saturday morning as Manny leaped onto the sideboard for the first leg of his journey to Daly City. It didn't look like a particularly good day for the beach. It was foggy but at least the weather wasn't cold.

Besides, Manny thought to himself, the fog will probably insure more privacy at the beach.

Manny was late arriving at Iris' as the BART train had broken down. It was already noon, and they were only half-way to their destination.

"How much further to the beach?"

"Not much further, Luv. Let me have another sip of that wine will you please?"

"Here. Did Kate tell you about the movie that some of the people at the gift shop are going to be in?" Manny asked.

"You mean the skin flick? Yes. She said I could be in it if I wanted."

"Are you going to, I am?"

"Not me, baby. When I break into films, it's going to be with my clothes on."

"You won't have to take your clothes off. It's a surrealistic film. Most of the people will be wearing costumes. I'm thinking about wearing my sailor outfit. It should be fun, why don't you try it?"

"Not me, Manny. You go ahead if you want to but count me out. Why don't you light up another joint?"

Iris drove out on a long peninsula and parked by a foggy beach. Manny grabbed the Frisbee from the back seat and tossed it to her. Between each toss of the Frisbee, the couple met to kiss. After one particularly long kiss, they put the toy down and walked quietly, arm in arm.

At the water's edge, Iris stooped to pick up a pretty shell or small pebble, while Manny watched the motion of the waves. Iris bent to pick up another stone that caught her eye. "Doesn't this look like a fetus?" She handed the stone to Manny.

The instant he saw he stone, a picture flashed in his mind.

"A fetus, a fetus, you said!" He saw his whole new book he was working on pass before his eyes.

The book would begin with a triangle of dots, and slowly the dots would evolve into the shape of a fetus. The fetus would give birth to the main character in the book. In the beginning, in the pre-birth stage, the character is told something, it is his mission to tell during his lifetime. The only trouble is daily existence keeps getting in the way of his completing the mission. He must tell; but he can't. Things keep getting in the way until it is almost too late, for the character is dying. Finally, as he is dying, he tells the people around him. The man then fades away into the triangle of dots.

"Fetus. That's it, Iris. In can do the book. I see it now. I know what I have to tell! I love you!"

THIRTY-FOUR

"Now Manny, as the scene begins, you start waltzing around the room with Sheila, here. Half-way through the dance, you start to slow down as she begins to fondle your cock and balls. Got it?"

"Sure, no problem." Manny was taking direction again; only this time instead of a monster movie, he was working on a triple X-rated film entitled 'Alice through the Wrong Looking Glass.'

True to her word, Kate, from the COMPLEX WEST gift shop, had landed him a part as an extra. Manny was thinking that this sure beat playing a monster for the little dictator, when the phone rang on the set. As luck would have it, the second lead's wife was calling to inform her actor-husband that if he didn't get home. pronto, she would leave him. This left a part to be filled; the circus strong man. The female director and producer, pressed for time, asked for volunteers. Manny's hand shot up like a schoolboy. After all, he had previous acting experience, and he could think of nothing more enjoyable than taking off his clothes and making love to the beautiful actress on his left.

Basically, his role as the strong man required he make love to three women in four separate scenes. The camera began to roll, and the fun began.

The first scene went fine. He had danced with Sheila and achieved the required erection as she fondled, and then went down on him. In the second scene, while Sheila was working on his cock, another actress approached him from the rear and began massaging his ass. Eventually she worked her way around and joined Sheila. Manny, in seventh heaven as the two women sucked his balls, was nearly oblivious to the scene around him, which included a man pedaling a bicycle, a fire-breather who nearly burned the hair off his chest, and a man in black leotards marching back and forth calling, "Time marches on."

The third scene was even more fun. It involved an orgy of people eating Kentucky Fried Chicken, drinking wine, smoking some of the best pot Manny had ever smoked, and screwing Alice. It wasn't until the last scene that the newly ordained porn star ran into problems.

As she set up the cameras, the director explained she wanted a good revealing shot. Manny could tell this would be something special by the way the crew quieted down in anticipation.

"All right, this is how the scene will work. First, Alice comes through the looking glass. She sees the strong man, that's you Manny, lying on the press bench pressing the barbells right here. The director pointed to the bench press table. As you press the weights up and down, the camera will pan down to a shot of Sheila going up and down on you. Got it"

"Sure, no problem." Manny took his place and began pressing the barbells. For once there was no noise on the set. Manny realized and tried to concentrate on what he was doing. In the meantime, Sheila was alternately giving him a hand job and sucking his cock to make sure he was good and hard.

"Good. Now Sheila, you stand up and get on top of him . . . Fine, now let's try the whole thing again."

Sheila remounted and began her up and down movements on Manny's cock. This time, unable to control himself, Manny began to cum. As the fluid shot out of him and into Sheila, he began to laugh. Soon, he was laughing so hard he couldn't stop.

"Cut!" Needless to say, the director and the crew were mad; "the entire shot has been ruined, yelled the director. We were supposed to film the cum shot!" But his anger was nothing compared to Sheila's hysterics.

"You bastard. I've never seen anything so unprofessional in my life. Don't you know you're not supposed to come inside of me?"

The more she screamed, the more Manny laughed, and soon tears began to stream down his face. Finally, he managed to control himself. "Sorry, I couldn't help it. No one told me I had to cum for the camera."

When the tired actor returned to the CRYSTAL TOWERS that night, he found Mury waiting for him at the door.

"Well, if it isn't the Portagee' movie star himself, home from a hard day on the set. How'd they like your sailor suit?"

"I never got to wear it." Manny launched into a detailed description of the day's events. "I even got paid."

"Great, sounds like you had a fantastic time. Too bad I won't be around to see the flick released."

"What do you mean?" asked Manny.

"This came in the mail today." Mury handed him a pretrial form he had to fill out. "Don't forget the trial is only a week away."

Sensing that his friend was upset, Manny tried to reassure him. "What are you worried about? Dr. Hank says he thinks you'll get off light. Didn't he say that because it was your first offense, you'd probably only get probation?"

Mury wouldn't be placated. "What if he's wrong? What if they put me in jail? I don't think I could take it."

"Mury, they won't put you in jail. Hank . . "

"I'm not taking any chances. I'm getting out of here. I'm all packed."

"Where the hell are you planning to go?"

"Arizona. They won't look for me out of state."

"I don't know what to say." Manny was surprised at Mury's decision. He never expected him to do anything but face the trial. Still, he could see that between his state, Mury was in and his stubborn Sagittarian streak. It was useless for him to argue.

"What do I tell Dr. Hank or the police if they come looking for you?"

"Tell them I went out, and you haven't heard from me. Tell them I'm never gone for more than a few days and will probably be back at any time. That should give me a head start."

"Okay, if that's what you really want. It's your life."

"Cheer up. You'd think you were the one going on the 'lam'."

"I'll go with you if you want."

"No. This is something I have to do alone. I'll drop you a line and let you know how I'm doing. Anyway, I need someone here to stall the police. Look . . . I have to leave before I change my mind. I've only been hanging around until you came home so I could say goodbye. See you around you little fucking Portagee'."

"Yah, see ya . . ."

THIRTY-FIVE

Manny didn't hear from Dr. Hank, the police, or Mury. He worried about his friend, and in order to distract his mind he devoted more time to his writing. The words were coming faster now, and he had an obsession to hurry and complete the work.

Susan had called to say she and the kids would be arriving May 14th. Manny could hardly wait. Each day he sent a picture drawing to show his children the places they would visit on their trip to San Francisco. He had told Iris of their visit and of his hope that she would meet his children. He was unprepared for her reaction.

The children, she had said, she would be glad to meet, but she simply couldn't understand why Susan was coming along or why Manny didn't divorce her. Manny tried to explain that divorce was expensive, and he didn't have any money. Iris was not sympathetic. She hinted that she might take a trip to Mexico around May 14th. Manny hoped she would change her mind, but all thoughts of them living together again were shelved until after Susan's visit. During dinner that night, the front door opened and in walked Mury. He had decided not to run away after all. He had been staying in Sacramento with his parents. Manny was delighted to see him. The two men embraced warmly.

"The trial is tomorrow."

"I know. Everything will be fine Mury."

*   *   *

The next morning Dr. Hank picked up Mury at the Crystal Towers apartment. It was agreed that Manny stay at home. Dr. Hank implied that until things were settled, the further he stayed away from court, the better.

It seemed to Manny as if the clock moved slowly that day. To pass the time, he sat on the balcony overlooking Alcatraz and San Francisco bay. He had counted eighty ships passing the old penitentiary and Mury still hadn't returned. It seemed ironic to Manny that while his friend was in court, he should be sitting and looking at Alcatraz. At five o'clock he heard a key in the door.

"Well?"

"Well?"

"Mury, how'd it go?"

"Not good, not bad."

"What the hell does that mean?"

"It means I pleaded guilty to a lesser charge. There weren't any witnesses and no cross examination, and it seemed quick."

"What about the sentence?"

"I don't know. Dr. Hank says it could be anything from probation to a year in jail. But one good thing happened; the forgery and embezzlement charges were dropped. Still, selling half an ounce of cocaine to narks is a hard charge to beat."

"What now?"

"I wait, but so far, so good. I feel like celebrating."

"Sounds good to me, let's go."

Their celebration consisted of drinks at the GALLEY IN THE ALLEY and a movie. The only item missing to make the evening complete was pot; something they hadn't been able to come by since the bust.

The next day, as if by magic, Iris called to say she was buying some "real good dope" from a friend and would they like her to pick up some for them.

"Would we? SSSSaaaaacccrrrmmmmentooooo . . . " Things were looking up

The next morning Manny called Iris to find out if the pot was in.

"I don't care whether it is or not, furthermore, I'm not planning to talk to you ever again."

Slam went the receiver. Iris had gone to the Ivory Tower again, and Manny couldn't understand why. After a week of trying to reach her via phone, he decided to go see her. Maybe she would talk to him in person. He had to knock three times before she would open the door.

"What's wrong?"

"Try asking Kate."

"Kate?"

"That's right." That was all Iris would say about the subject. The only thing Manny could think of was that Kate had told Iris about their one night stand.

As quickly as her anger had flared up, it disappeared. They were lovers once again. A few days later Manny was at Iris's apartment for drinks. He asked her once more about the pot. She told him she had only been able to buy one ounce, and that was for herself, and she didn't know when her source would be able to get more. Later that night, as Manny went to the freezer to get ice for their drinks, he notice a second packet of grass tucked in the corner. He didn't say anything to Iris. He merely stored the information in his head, but he was hurt. Later that week Manny mentioned the incident to Mury, who said nothing, but only shook his head. It wasn't until the following week that things came to a head.

It started at dinner, Manny informed Mury that Iris would be coming over for drinks Wednesday night. Mury hit the ceiling.

"I don't believe it. First, she hangs up on you; then she lies about the dope. How much abuse are you going to take from that bitch? I don't want her in this apartment. You may be crazy, but I'm not!"

Iris did come on Wednesday and stayed until Thursday. That morning at breakfast, Mury told Manny he was moving out. One thing led to another and soon a heated argument was in progress. Mury indirectly said something about Iris, and before he could stop himself, Manny said that poetry had been ruined by homosexuals. It was the first time Manny had ever attached Mury on the subject, and Mury was hurt.

Over the next week things were strained between the roommates. Manny apologized for his comment and had taken Mury out for a drink to make amends. The relationship seemed to be on the mend, but Mury still planned to move out. He felt sure he would be in jail by June and didn't want to waste a whole month's rent. That left Manny concerned about money. He couldn't afford the entire rent alone, and wondered where he would live. Moving back in with Iris was one solution. Still, even there he would need money, and money was a problem for more than one reason. His unemployment checks still hadn't arrived and Susan was due on Sunday. Like it or not, he would have to call and ask her to bring along some extra cash.

"Hello."

"Hi Susan. It's me."

"Hi."

"I just called to see if everything is all set for Sunday. I can't wait to see all of you."

"We can't wait to see all of you either. The kids are so excited. Google is telling all his friends about the big jet plane he's going on."

"What time will you be arriving?"

"We'll be in at 8:50 on flight 720."

"Is it a direct flight?"

"No. We have to make a few stops. Have your unemployment checks come yet?"

"Well . . . that's one of the reasons I called. They haven't come in, and since I really don't have the money to take you to the places I'd like to go. I was hoping you could bring some money along. I figure a hundred would get us through if we took it easy."

"A hundred dollars! You told me I wouldn't have to spend a cent on this trip. I don't know if I even want to come out there now."

"You don't want to come! I just spent six hundred dollars on those lousy tickets. That's all the money I had in the world."

"I don't care. You told me I wouldn't have to pay for a thing. I can't afford to be taking money out of the bank for this trip. I don't know if I want to come."

"Don't come if that's the way you feel about it! I can use the six hundred dollars!" Slam went the receiver.

Manny could not help but yell. "Damn that fucking bitch. Ball busters, they're all ball busters. Jesus, I've got to talk to somebody. Maybe Iris is home."

"Hello, Iris Ivory here."

"Iris, its Manny."

"Hi Manny, how are you? All set for the kids to come?"

"They're not coming. Susan is bullshit because my unemployment checks didn't arrive."

Iris was not sympathetic. Instead, she reminded Manny that he should have divorced Susan long ago. They had a fight which ended up with Iris telling him she planned to go to Mexico with Gail.

Manny didn't know what to do next. He was beside himself with anguish. For weeks he had looked forward to seeing his children. He picked up the phone once more. "It's me again, Susan."

"What do you want?"

"I have to see the kids. I can't tell you how much I've looked forward to all of you coming; how many times I've cried over their pictures. You have to come out. Maybe my checks will arrive while you're here. If they do, I'll pay you back. I'm asking you once more, please come."

"I don't know. I'll have to think about it."

"When will I know?"

"When the plane lands."

THIRTY-SIX

~~~~~~

It was eight-thirty when Manny arrived at San Francisco International Airport. He checked with American information desk and learned that Flight 720 would arrive at 8:50, right on time. His only question was, would Susan and the kids be on it?

He took his time finding gate fourteen. The twenty minute wait was passed watching the pretty women and observing the people greeting their friends and relatives. Before he knew it, a PA system came to life: FLIGHT NUMBER SEVEN TWENTY IS NOW ARRIVING AT GATE NUMBER FOURTEEN. The pace of Manny's heart quickened.

The minutes seemed like hours as he stood watching the big jet taxi to the gate and make preparations for the bridge like telescope to allow its passengers to disembark. He wondered what happened to the days when you could watch passengers coming down the plane's steps. If Susan and the kids were on the plane, Manny wouldn't know until they crossed the threshold into the terminal, itself.

Several men came through the tunnel. Manny thought they looked like businessmen rushing to their next appointment. Straining to see down the long tunnel, he caught a glimpse of a woman with a child. As the figures moved closer, he could see it wasn't his family. Soon more people hurried into the waiting area and into the arms of friends and lovers. The crowd began to thin. Just then he spotted a little boy running in his direction. His hopes rose. As the boy approached, Manny began to hold out his arms.

"Daddy." A man in a blue suit embraced his boy.

I'm not leaving until the last person is off that plane, Manny thought to himself.

Nearly at the point of giving up, Manny watched as the last good-sized crowd of people came into view. It was then he saw them; two sleepy children holding onto a woman in a tan raincoat. The woman was smiling at him. It was Susan, and she had come.

"You made it. I was afraid you weren't coming. Come here you two little piggys; Daddy wants to give you a big hug and kiss. One for your mommy, too."

"Hello Manny."

"Hello Susan. It's good to see you."

"It's good to see you too."

Picking up both children he asked Susan, "Did you have any trouble on the flight?"

"None. It was a long ride, but the kids were good. They slept most of the way. Have you been waiting long?"

"Not really. I hope you don't mind a bus ride into town. I had planned on borrowing Iris's car, she's the woman I wrote you about, but she went to Mexico."

"I don't mind the bus as long as the ride isn't too long. I'm exhausted."

"It's only about twenty minutes to downtown San Francisco by bus, and from there, a five minutes to my apartment by cab. You can see some of the city during the ride."

As they rode, Manny caught up on news of his family and pointed out the sights to his children. When they arrived at the Crystal Towers, Mury was ready with the customary bottle of champagne and a palm reading.

Susan took to Mury immediately, as did the children. If Manny wasn't assured of his friend's homosexuality, he might have been jealous, as he had been on other occasions when women paid more attention to Mury than him. The evening passed rapidly with light conversation and when it was time for bed; Mury offered his big double bed to Susan and Manny.

The next two weeks seemed to Manny like pages from a San Francisco travel folder. He took his family everywhere; everywhere that didn't cost too much money. His unemployment checks still hadn't arrived.

Still, money didn't spoil the visit, and Susan seemed to enjoy the city as much as he did. She loved it. They visited all the large hotels and even took a ride in the open elevator at the Hyatt Regency. The kids especially liked watching the seals at Seal Rock. Mury offered to babysit on several nights, and Manny took Susan to some of his favorite night spots. Their personal relationship wasn't going as well as the vacation. Susan seemed reserved and cool toward him. He couldn't put his finger on what was bothering her, although he suspected it was a strong resentment about his leaving Massachusetts to come out west. Several times Manny tried to get Susan to talk about her anger, hoping that the air world be cleared between the two of them, but she always changed the subject. Interestingly enough, the fight that was inevitable between he and Susan, was triggered by another woman.

Iris had returned from Mexico the last day of the family visit. That morning she called Manny and asked to meet his family. She also asked if she could take his children out for an ice cream. Manny didn't see any harm in inviting her over. After all, Susan had met several of his women friends since their separation, and even, on occasion, had lunch with Miranda, but he wasn't ready for Susan's reaction as Iris walked in the front door.

Susan retreated to her own personal Ivory Tower. She refused to get off the sofa to greet Iris and sat crying. Manny, unsure of how to handle the situation ushered Iris and the kids out the door, leaving Susan sulking on the couch. He would face her later.

Iris looked tanned and rested from her trip. There wasn't much time for Manny to talk to her with the kids tugging on his sleeve and asking for more ice cream, but he did manage to tell her that Mury was definitely moving out. He asked what she thought about their living together. Iris hesitated, and said she would have to think about it. Something about Iris was different, but Manny couldn't put his finger on what the change was. He wondered if something had happened in Mexico, but there was no time to worry about it now. Manny had other problems. It was time to head home to Susan.

Riding up in the elevator, Manny steeled himself to do battle with Susan. Surprisingly, the battle was mild. Susan had regained her composure and indicated she had begun to accept Manny's new life. She told him what upset her the most, was the fact that Iris had intruded on the family's last day together.

Later, walking to the Basque Restaurant in North Beach for their farewell dinner, they discussed their mutual respect and love for each other. Even if they couldn't be husband and wife, they would always be friends.

Over a delicious roast beef dinner, Manny and Susan discussed their respective plans. She was planning to go back to teaching. Manny told her he was planning to move back in with Iris.

"I think living with Iris might be difficult," Susan said. "She strikes as a woman who wants her own way."

"She is. I know I'm going to have to make a lot of concessions. Even though I'll be collecting unemployment, I know she'll put pressure on me to get some kind of job. She doesn't consider writing work, and she thinks anyone who doesn't have a job is lazy."

"Well, all I can say is good luck."

Savoring their last glimpse of San Francisco together, the group walked back to the CRYSTAL TOWERS to pick up the luggage. Mury was waiting with a going away present for Susan; a pancake griddle that she had admired. He always gave away those things of his that people admired.

"Thank you, Mury for everything, Susan said hefting the griddle. And good luck with your sentencing." Manny ushered the group out the door for their last cable car ride in San Francisco. As the car climber half-way to the stars, no one notice that one star in particular was not so faint that it could only be observed with a telescope. It was Kohoutek. Its presence was still being felt, but it was almost gone.

THIRTY-SEVEN

Manny had arrived in San Francisco in November and it was now the ninth of June; the day of Mury's sentencing. "The day of reckoning," as Iris had called it that morning. As planned, Manny was living with his lady love in Daly City. That morning he had come back to the CRYSTAL TOWERS to wait for Mury's return from court. Mury had said he wanted to break the news to him personally and at the same time also pick up some money Manny owed him as Manny's unemployment checks had finally come through. At three o'clock footsteps were heard on the stairs. Manny was waiting at the door.

"Well?"

"Three months in a fire conservation corps."

"Oh. . . ." Even if it didn't sound like jail, in essence that's what it was. "When do you have to go?"

"The seventeenth. One more week of freedom." Mury's laugh didn't sound very convincing.

Manny didn't know exactly what to say. "I know this is going to sound strange, Mury, especially since I'm not the one who has to go to jail. But in some ways I don't regret any of it. It was one hell of an adventure."

"I know what you mean. Probably, if I'd shown remorse the judge would have given me probation, but . . . well, I still don't think we did anything wrong. I was trying to make money for Sourdough Sam's, and the things we believed in and no court can change my convictions and make me feel like a criminal."

The two friends spent the afternoon discussing Manny's book and his relationship with Iris. Manny told Mury that their first week of living together had not been very successful. In fact, it was a repeat of their last living arrangement. Iris still resented having his things in her space.

Furthermore, she felt she deserved to have a famous author for a lover, not a would-be writer. She had no understanding that to become successful, Manny would first have to write a book.

"It's a frustrating situation, and I didn't know what to do. I can't live with her, and I can't live without her." Manny's head dropped as he opened the door to head back to Daly City.

*   *   *

At Iris' apartment, Manny heard her car pull into the garage. She was home from work early, and Manny wondered if that meant she was in a good mood, or a bad mood. Fortunately, when he opened the door, it was Michelle who entered.

Greeting Mury warmly with a kiss and a hug, she insisted she invite some people over for a little party. Manny watched in amazement as she picked up the phone and invited Mury, Bobby, and Gail over for drinks and smoke.

"What are you staring at, Luv. I thought it would be nice to have reunion."

The night was one of fun and memories. The group hadn't been together since Mury's Christmas party when Manny and Iris pulled their role switch. Tonight they seemed so close together and yet so separate in themselves.

Mury, of course, would be going to jail in a week. Still, he seemed full of life and searching for a new direction. Gail had a new job and a new apartment, this time without roommate, and Bobby, although still with his old insurance job, had a new boyfriend and a new tape for his car.

Listening to 'Love Unlimited,' for old times' sake, the group sat on the waterbed smoking and drinking until the wee hours of the morning. As Gail and Bobby said their farewells, Mury stretched out on the bearskin rug in the living room. Calling a blessing to Iris and Manny as they retired to the bedroom, he quickly turned over and went to sleep.

In the bedroom, Iris and Manny made love. It was only their second lovemaking since they moved back in together. Despite the strain in their relationship, they drifted off to sleep that night believing it just might be possible to put things back together.

THIRTY-EIGHT

"Tap . . . Tap . . . tap . . . tap, tap, tap! "That's the last of it, I'm done. I did it. The book is finished," Manny yelled.

Manny then sat quietly for a moment and looked at the pages he had just typed. No one else ever wrote this book; the idea is totally mine, he thought. All those words; all those notes creating pictures. He ran to the window and flung it open.

"Listen all you people out there in Daly City, all you cars on the highway, all you houses on the hill, I'm done! I'm an author. I finished the BOOK."

Suddenly he was silent. Five months of work. Of course, he knew he still had a lot left to do. There was the revising, the editing, and the search for a publisher, but still, he was proud of himself and shouted it at the rooftops. "I'm a fucking author. I finished!" Iris, he thought to himself. Maybe now she'll feel better about my writing. Maybe she'll think the book has potential.

Manny poured himself some bourbon, toasted himself, and sat on the armchair. He wished Iris would come home. He wanted to share his triumph with someone. He thought about the last two weeks of living together

"On second thought," he said, "maybe it's better she isn't here."

Iris had been extremely bitchy lately. She had almost nothing good to say to him anymore. He thought about her reaction to the letter he had received from his lawyer requesting his power of attorney so the papers could be signed for the sale of his house in Bedford Farms. He was looking for a little sympathy. He felt bad the house had to go on the market. Iris however, merely shrugged her shoulders and walked in the other room.

Thoughts of the house temporarily deflated his mood of celebration, especially since the lawyer who was handling the sale was a good friend of Lenny Solens. Manny knew he would get screwed.

Trying to look on the bright side, Manny reminded himself that the sale of the house would lift a bit responsibility from his shoulders. Now he could do whatever he wanted without worrying where his next mortgage payment would come from. Of course, since he still owed twenty-six hundred dollars in missed payments, he wouldn't make any money on the sale.

Who cares? He figured. It's a weight off my mind. Besides, I'm an author, and today I should be celebrating."

He rose and poured himself another drink. Crossing to the desk, he took one more look at his masterpiece. His good mood was restored and once more he shouted out the window:

"The book is done! I'm finished. I did it!"

THIRTY-NINE

Three days had passed since Manny finished the book, and he had lost his good mood. He sat on the chair, jumped up, paced back and forth across the living room and returned to the chair once again. He was furious at Iris.

Three days he had waited for some word of congratulations and still nothing. She acted as if people she knew finished books every day. To make things worse, she had suggested it was time for him to go out and get a real job like everyone else. When he had tried to explain to her about things like revisions and editing, she had given him a murderous look. Sometimes he didn't know what she expected from him. But of course, in reality he did know what she wanted, for she had told him often enough.

"I want someone who will take care of me. I'm tired of feeding myself and keeping a roof over my head."

Manny didn't understand why she had to keep bugging him about a job. He paid his half of the rent and shared the household tasks. Lately, she had even started bugging him about needing some freedom to go out alone at night. Manny had told her to go ahead; that no one was holding her prisoner in the apartment.

Something told Manny that her desires to get out of the house had something to do with meeting other men. Iris had told him that during her trip to Mexico, she had met this fantastic, incredible guy named Jeff. He thought he would never hear the end of her stories about how this twenty-four year old kid had screwed her on some beach.

"It was soooooo romantic." Iris had even dragged him to a beach on the coast to try and repeat the episode with Manny. As they had finished their lovemaking, Manny had looked up the clift along the road. He flinched when he saw a crowd of people staring down at them. He was positive she had set up the entire situation to relive her Mexican fantasy. To make matters worse, Manny had been sunburned that afternoon on his exposed crotch. Memories of the afternoon triggered Manny's anger and frustration. He began his pacing once more. He didn't know how much longer he could live like this. Maybe Mury was right about Iris.

The more he paced, the more he had a desire to get out of the apartment. He thought of the four hundred dollars he had tucked in the bank. He could take that money and head down to the Yucatan to look for the evidence of Atlanteans were supposed to have etched on the pyramids. He had read about it through Edgar Cayce. Or he could buy a used car and drive around the country. Of course, four hundred dollars wasn't a lot of money, but it could buy him a ticket someplace. Maybe Rome; but if he went to Rome, he would have to stop off in Massachusetts and say goodbye to his family. He thought of his brother Dave.

"Carrumba, I'm going to give Dave a call," Manny said out loud. He went to the phone and dialed the number.

"Dave, it's your brother."

"Manny! Where the hell are you? Everyone has been upset since we heard you were going to jail."

"I'm not going to jail. That was my friend, Mury. As a matter of fact, he went yesterday; but it wasn't really jail, just some fire conservation corps. There was a drug deal, a cocaine deal, but I was never questioned about it. I'm fine."

"I'm glad to hear that. What are you doing out there?"

"I just finished my first book, and I'm living with this chick, Iris. I've been thinking about coming home through, and then going to Rome, or someplace like that. To write . . . What do you think?"

"I think you should come home. Everybody wants you here."

"Well, I'm thinking about it, but I haven't made up my mind yet. How's Dad?"

"Fine now, but you should have heard him when Susan told him you were in jail. He called me up and blasted me out for not knowing what was going on in California. He even started trying to dig up money for bail."

"Well, I hope he knows by now that I'm not in any trouble."

"Susan went over and talked to him after she got back from California. Everybody was a little confused about the story, but I think he's reassured. I hope you decide to come home, Manny."

"I'll think about it. Listen, I have to go now. You know how much these long distance calls cost. Say hello to everyone for me, will yah?"

"I will, and take it easy."

It felt good talking to David. It pleased Manny to hear his family missed him. Maybe I should go home. He started pacing. He thought of his time in San Francisco and of the things that had happened. He had come to write a book and he had done it. Not the book he planned to write, but he had written his first book.

Mury was in jail, and all that was left was Iris. The thought of Iris made Manny angry again. He loved her, but she hurt him over and over. He had to get rid of some of the anger he was feeling. He crossed to the typewriter.

"How could I love you so much when I hate you so much?
You take me and tear me and throw me up in the air
and make me feel like a little kid, but I love you.
I could tear you apart with my bare hands but
all I want to do is take you in my arms.
I don't think I can stand it much longer.
I'm getting torn to pieces.
I hate the thought of just being one of your memories.
I hate the thought of being far away from you.
What the hell are you doing to me?
You're making me act like a fifteen-year-old."

FORTY

"Hey Luv. Come on, wake up. Its nine o'clock and I have to leave for work. Do you want me to make you a cup of tea before I go?"

"No thanks. I'll have one after I eat. Did you have a good time last night?"

"Oh, so-so." Iris added, "I didn't get in until late so I didn't bother to wake you."

"Yah, I kind of guessed that."

"Listen Luv, I have to run now, but I might be home early. See you later and don't forget to do the laundry. You know where the change is."

"Yah, I know. See ya' later." See you much later, Manny thought to himself. He had to get out of there; he couldn't take it anymore. In fact, he world go that very day.

Manny spent the morning eating, and mulling over his problems. By noontime he began to call airlines to find out which one had the best deal.

". . . and thank you for calling American." Manny hung up the phone just as Iris walked through the door.

"You're home early."

"I told you I might be. Who was on the phone?"

"American Airlines."

"The airline? What did they call for?"

"There didn't call me. I called them."

"What for?"

"I'm leaving today on a two o'clock flight. What do you think about it?"

"Hey, it's your life baby."

"That's how I feel, too. Can I borrow a suitcase? I'll mail it back to you."

"Sure. You can use the old white one. Can I help you pack?"

"No thanks, but I would appreciate you driving me to the bank and then out to the airport."

"Sure."

That was it; it was over. No tears or screaming; no angry words or recriminations. As Manny packed, he turned off his feelings and went into neutral. In an hour, he was ready to go.

Iris dropped him off in front of the American terminal. They kissed, and he handed her a twenty dollar bill to cover his half of the month's phone bill. Brushing away the approaching skycap, he carried his worldly possessions through the automatic doors. They consisted of two suitcases and four small boxes.

Manny was still in emotional neutral when the stewardess came to ask him what he wanted to drink.

"A Grandad' on the rocks, please."

The only other thing Manny later recalled about the flight was the announcement that came over the intercom:

"THIS IS THE CAPATAIN SPEAKING. WELCOME ABOARD FLIGHT 222 FROM SAN FRANCISCO TO BOSTON. WE ARE CRUISING AT AN APPROZIMATE SPEED OF 600 MILES PER HOUR. AT AN ALATITUDE OF THIRTY THOUSAND FEET. ESTIMATED TIME OF ARRIVAL IN BOSTON IS TWELVE O' FIVE P.M. THE WEATHER IS BOSTON IS CLEAR AND WARM. I WILL TURN ON THE SMOKING LIGHT IN FIVE MINUTES. HAVE A NICE FLIGHT AND THANK YOU FOR FLYING AMERICAN."

EPILOGUE

The following article was clipped from the LOWELL SUN newspaper on June 18, 1975.

HALLEY'S COMET MAY BE 1986 FLOP
By Warren E. Leary

"CAMBRIDGE, MASS. (AP) – Astronomers say people awaiting the return of Halley's Comet in 1986 shouldn't expect a celestial extravaganza. It might be another Kohoutek.

Two comet experts say the interplay of several factors probably will dull the greatly anticipated return of the world's most popular comet, last seen in 1910. This could mean Halley will be no more spectacular that last year's disappointing Comet Kohoutek.

The latest orbital calculations indicate Halley's Comet will pass almost three times further away from earth than on its previous visit, the astronomers say. To complicate things even further, the comet's greatest brightness and longest tail will occur below the plane of the earth's equator, making seeing it from the Northern Hemisphere more difficult and less exciting, they say.

"We merely remark that if you were disappointed by Comet Kohoutek in early 1974, don't have high hopes for a fine display of Comet Halley."

*　　*　　*

Three weeks after he returned home, Manny was fishing on the pier at the family cottage. Suddenly he heard footsteps behind him and turned to find his cousin Al on the pier, walking towards him.

"How you doing Manny? Did you get out of that San Francisco scrape alright?"

"Sure Al. No problems here, except my pal had to do a little time in a conservation camp. But I made it back without a scratch. How about you?"

"I'm doing alright. I just wanted to check on you. I've got to get back up to the cottage now; hot dogs on the grill. See you soon. And don't let one of those big fish pull you in."

Manny watched his cousin walk off the pier and up the hill. It was the last time he saw Al. Two weeks later Manny got a call from Al's younger brother. He wanted to know if Manny had a passport and if Al could borrow it to get out of the country. Manny answered, no, he had no passport. Not long after, Al's car was found abandoned at Logan Airport. A while after the car was found; Al's father got a call from a stranger. He was told the father that his son, Al was at the bottom of a lake somewhere in New Hampshire.

A year after his cousin Al went missing; Manny Silva got many small jobs including as a male exotic dancer in order to keep writing. Eventually Manny got a notice from the Veterans Administration that he was deemed disabled with Post Traumatic Stress Syndrome, (PTSD), due to his time spent in the Vietnam War. With the Disability came four more years of schooling. Manny attended Boston University and got a degree in Communications. He continued his writing.

www.ingramcontent.com/pod-product-compliance
Lightning Source LLC
Chambersburg PA
CBHW060504130626
46553CB00002B/407